Textile Masterpieces of Ancient Peru

WITH 77 ILLUSTRATIONS IN FULL COLOR

by

James W. Reid

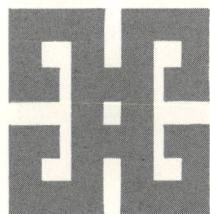

DOVER PUBLICATIONS, INC.
NEW YORK

Credits and Acknowledgments

Particular thanks are due to the private collectors throughout the world for their cooperation in providing reproductions of their textiles. As a result of their gracious assistance, it has been possible to use numerous illustrations of pieces never before reproduced.

The following institutions, and/or directors thereof, were also especially generous in kindly seeking out and furnishing examples of exceptional textiles from their archives: Vladimir Haustov, Martin and Ullman ArtWeave Textile Gallery, New York; Jonathan Hill, Hill Ethnic Textiles, San Francisco; José Antonio de Lavalle, Ediciones L. L. Lavalle, Banco de Crédito, Lima, Peru; Gail Martin, Martin and Ullman ArtWeave Textile Gallery, New York; Edward H. Merrin, Edward H. Merrin Gallery, New York; Andrés Moraga, Moraga/Daniel Collection, San Francisco; Museo Nacional de Antropología y Arqueología, Lima, Peru; Museo Julio C. Tello del Sitio, Paracas, Peru; Linda Schildkraut, Edward H. Merrin Gallery, New York; Öcr Ullman, Martin and Ullman ArtWeave Textile Gallery, New York.

Institutional Credits for Color Illustrations: Hill Ethnic Textiles, 45; Martin and Ullman ArtWeave Textile Gallery, 30, 44, 53, 56, 65, 67, 68, 72, 74; Edward H. Merrin Gallery, 27, 28, 37, 60, 70, 71; Moraga/Daniel Collection, 64; Museo Nacional de Antropología y Arqueología, Lima, 2, 3, 4, 5, 6, 7, 8, 9, 36; Museo Julio C. Tello, Paracas, 42. All others: private collections (E. Poli: 24, 26, 43, 47).

Photographic Credits: Fred Allert, 16, 21, 24, 25, 26, 38, 43, 57, 75, 77; José Luis Catalina, 54; Jian Chen, 1, 12, 13, 18, 19, 20, 22, 23, 31, 32, 33, 34, 35, 39, 40, 42, 46, 48, 51, 55, 59, 61, 63, 66, 69; Javier Ferran, 11, 14, 15, 70; Justin Kerr, 27, 28, 37, 60, 62, 71; Werner Lange, 2, 3, 4, 5, 6, 7, 8, 9, 36; Alcides Perucca, 29, 41; Lyle Wachovsky, 30, 44, 53, 56, 65, 67, 68, 72, 73, 74; Enrique Wong, 10.

Photograph of Author: Lyle Wachovsky.

Map Design: José Carnero.

Published in Canada by General Publishing Company, Ltd., 30 Lesmill Road, Don Mills, Toronto, Ontario.

Published in the United Kingdom by Constable and Company, Ltd., 10 Orange Street, London WC2H 7EG.

Textile Masterpieces of Ancient Peru: With 77 Illustrations in Full Color is a new work, first published by Dover Publications, Inc., in 1986.

Manufactured in the United States of America
Dover Publications, Inc., 31 East 2nd Street, Mineola, N.Y. 11501

Library of Congress Cataloging-in-Publication Data

Reid, James W.
Textile masterpieces of ancient Peru.

Includes bibliographical references.
1. Indians of South America—Peru—Textile industry and fabrics.   I. Title.
F3429.3.T3R45   1986   746′.0985   86-24042
ISBN 0-486-25246-9

INTRODUCTION

PART I: **THE TEXTILES AND THEIR HISTORICAL BACKGROUND**

Their Appreciation as Art from the Conquest to the Present Day

When Francisco Pizarro, with 110 footsoldiers and 67 horse, arrived in the northern Peruvian mountain town of Cajamarca in November 1532, the Spaniards were astounded by the textiles. "One can only marvel at the way they are made," commented Pedro Pizarro, brother of the conquistador, while the chronicler Francisco de Xeres was equally enthusiastic: "It is wonderful how highly the cloth is prized in Spain for its workmanship. It is looked upon more as silk than as wool."[1]

These were generous words from men who found the local beliefs pagan and abhorrent to their militant catholicism, and it says a great deal for these ancient textiles that their beauty was not lost upon these hardened adventurers. For some two thousand years before the Conquest, along the Pacific desert coast, in remote Andean valleys and amid the sweeping expanses of the bleak, steppe-like *altiplano* (Sp),* weavers produced textiles of incomparable technical skill and startling aesthetic beauty. Although destined for many uses, they were fundamentally religious in inspiration and content, created to express a faith which the extirpators of idolatries in the service of the Spanish viceroys could not tolerate.

Thus it was that, as the Spanish regime systematically crushed the religion, as well as the social, political and economic structures of the Andean world, it not only annulled the immense Inca empire, which included all of present-day Peru, Bolivia and Ecuador, as well as large sections of Colombia, Argentina and Chile: it also insured the demise of weaving as a creative art, the disappearance of what the Chilean poet Pablo Neruda has called "radiant cloth" from the "golden thread of the vicuña, to attire the loves, the burial sites, the mothers, the king, the prayers and the warriors" of those resplendent pre-Columbian cultures of ancient Peru.[2]

*Terms followed by "(Sp)" are in Spanish rather than in an indigenous Indian language. The altiplano is the flat, plateau-like area, about 13,000 feet in altitude, which is one of the geographic components of the Highland zone; it is primarily located in Bolivia. Other areas are the high valleys and mountains.

If their weavings have survived in surprisingly large quantities, and often in perfect condition, it is because of two felicitous circumstances—the elaborate original burial rituals and the ideal conditions for conservation on the dry Pacific coast, where the majority of the tombs were located. Much of the coast had changed little since the time of the Conquest when the French traveler Paul Marcoy described it in his classic work published in 1872:

> From north to south nothing is visible but sand dunes and craggy cliffs, shores strewn with driftwood, long stretches of saltpeter and sea salt, heaps of calcareous deposits, stony islets covered with guano[3] and rocks of all forms and colors. The purity of the air, the intensity of the light, the unalterable blue of sea and sky, bring out in sharp relief all the details of the weird scenery and, leaving none of its features in shadow, impress the beholder with a sense of blinding immensity, of melancholy splendor and implacable repose.[4]

The Spaniards sent samples of Peruvian archeological objects to Charles V in the mid-sixteenth century, and the Frenchman Dombey introduced Peruvian artifacts to the Cabinet des Médailles in Paris in the 1700s.[5] However, the scope and significance of ancient Peruvian textiles, ceramics and objects of metal, wood and stone were generally ignored until the mid-nineteenth century. At that time, a series of explorers and archeologists began to reveal to Western Europe and North America the legacy of artistic treasures bequeathed to posterity by pre-Conquest Peru. The most prominent figures were the Germans Reiss, Stübel, Baessler and Uhle; the Frenchmen Marcoy, d'Orbigny and Wiener; and the American Squier.

In the first decades of the 1900s, while the German Arthur Posnansky was making his initial investigations of the great site of Tiahuanaco, in highland Bolivia, the first significant appraisals of ancient Peruvian textiles began to appear. In the United States, M. D. C. Crawford and Charles Mead made notable contributions. In 1916 Crawford wrote: "In Peru, textiles reached their highest development. The harmony of color, the beauty and fastness of dyes and the perfection of weaving place these fabrics in a class by themselves."[6] Subsequently, major contributions related to their technical attributes were made by the Frenchman Raoul d'Harcourt, and in anthropological and archeological

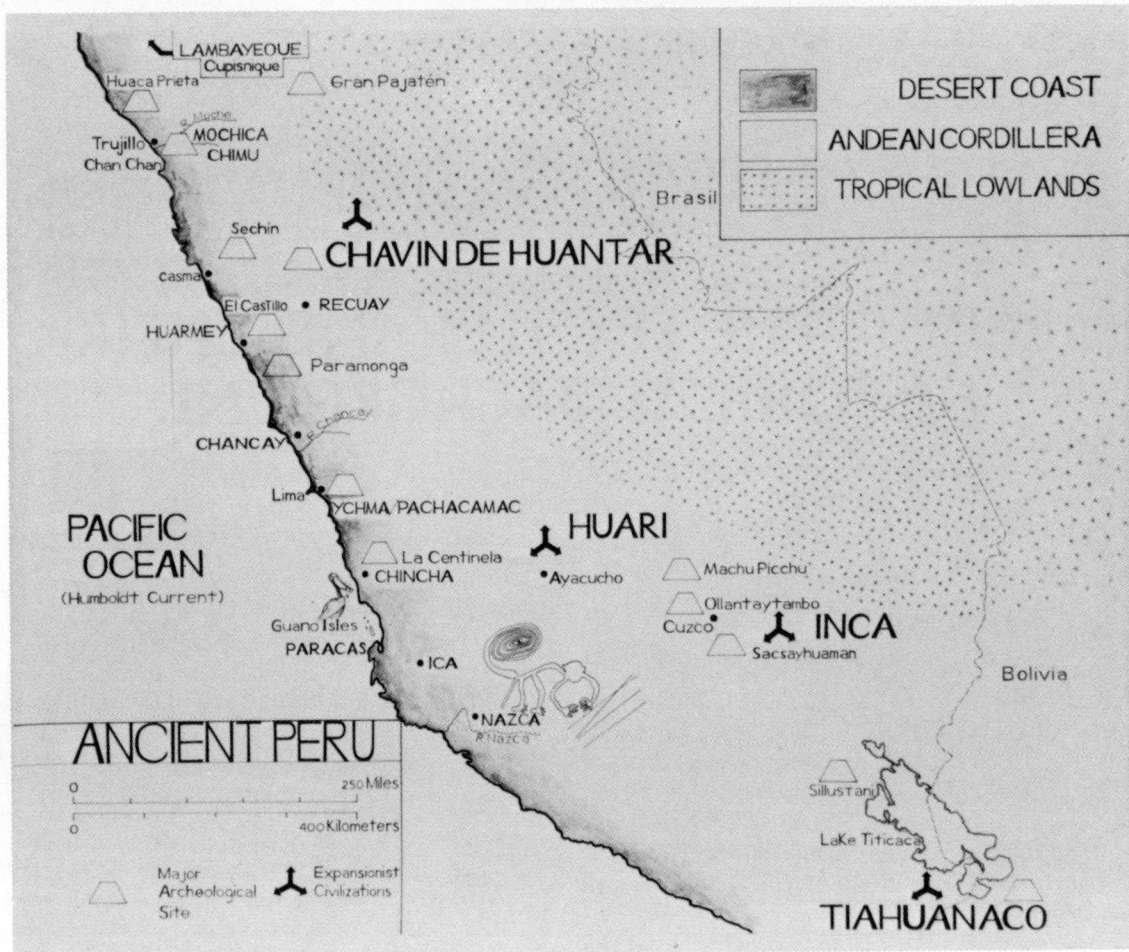

LAMBAYEQUE
Cupisnique
Huaca Prieta
Gran Pajatén
Brasil

DESERT COAST
ANDEAN CORDILLERA
TROPICAL LOWLANDS

Trujillo
Chan Chan
MOCHICA
CHIMU
Sechin
CHAVIN DE HUANTAR
casma
El Castillo • RECUAY
HUARMEY
Paramonga
CHANCAY
Lima
YCHMA PACHACAMAC
HUARI
PACIFIC
OCEAN
(Humboldt Current)
La Centinela
CHINCHA
•Ayacucho
Machu Picchu
Ollantaytambo
Cuzco
INCA
Sacsayhuaman
Guano Isles
PARACAS
• ICA
•NAZCA
Nazca
Bolivia

ANCIENT PERU
0   250 Miles
0   400 Kilometers

Sillustani
Lake Titicaca
TIAHUANACO

Major
Archeological
Site
Expansionist
Civilizations

studies by the Americans Wendell Bennett, Junius Bird, Alan Sawyer, John H. Rowe, Ann P. Rowe, Jane P. Dwyer, Irene Emery, Mary Elizabeth King and William J. Conklin.

Although Leroy Appleton noted in 1950 that "no people in the history of fabric-making have ever . . . excelled these people in either design or color,"[7] and although the late New York art dealer John Wise arranged textile exhibitions from the 1930s on, the emphasis in museum curatorial activities, seminars, round-table discussions and displays continued to be upon technical and archeological facets. Major U.S. exhibitions—that of 1954 at The Museum of Modern Art in New York entitled "Ancient Art of the Andes," that of 1961 organized by Junius Bird at the American Museum of Natural History and dedicated to "Art and Life in Old Peru," and the 1969-70 Peruvian loan exhibitions of "Master-Craftsmen of Ancient Peru" shown at the Los Angeles County Museum and the Guggenheim Museum in New York—generally presented textiles as part of an archeological environment. Major exhibitions of the past decade—the 1979 "Warp and Weft Patterns of the Andes" and the 1984 "Costumes and Featherwork of the Lords of Chimor, Textiles from Peru's North Coast," both admirably curated by Ann P. Rowe of the Textile Museum in Washington, D.C.—have further elaborated upon this tradition, as well as making significant new contributions.

Apart from a handful of superb exhibitions organized in the past twenty years by several imaginative New York art galleries, very little attention has been dedicated to the aesthetic importance of ancient Peruvian textiles as art works per se. This oversight is all the more remarkable because of their glowing colors, boldly conceived compositions, often highly cerebral iconography and virtuoso linear calligraphy. These factors, combined with their affinities with so much of twentieth-century art, fully vindicate their right to be considered as creative art works in their own right.

This is not to diminish their technical attributes, or their "psychological" relevance as objects of notable religious, social, political, economic and shamanistic impact. Writing of African art in 1926, Dr. J. Maes, an early authority at the Congo Museum in Brussels, noted that its true beauty would be appreciated only if we understood its psychology; only with an understanding of its sense, its significance and the reason for its existence would it be possible to penetrate all its beauty and all its life.[8] So it is with Peruvian textile art. It too is rich in symbolism, in ritual, in magic, in mystery and in mythology; it also is steeped in religious faith, imbued with a profound sense of the cosmic and the divine, and infused with a constant awareness of the synergistic ties between gods and mortals. Ancient Peruvian textiles derive from and reflect the world-view of Andean man. As such, they are an expression of his beliefs, visual metaphors to communicate

4

deeply felt credos in a world that had no writing as we think of it.

Nor did it have the sort of documented information that has helped to clarify the development of Western civilization. The Andean world had no Bible, no illuminated manuscripts, no written information recorded on tablets, scrolls or codices, and very few confirmed historical facts. The Spanish chroniclers provide firsthand information about both the Incas and the peoples who had been subjugated by them since the Inca Pachacutec initiated a program of imperial expansion in the mid-fifteenth century.[9] Some of this material is evidently subjective, especially when religion is concerned, but many of the observations—those dealing with patterns of daily existence, for example—have a definite ring of truth to them.

The Andean world, especially the highland area, resists change even now, so that much of what the chroniclers tell us about weaving in the Inca period was probably quite similar to what had occurred in the preceding two thousand years. The Inca system of what amounted to state socialism, its authoritarian, structured organization and its meticulous planning probably institutionalized the weaving process to an unprecedented degree; but the fundamental raison d'être and modus operandi of the weaver in all likelihood differed very little from that of his counterparts centuries before.

The Gods and Their Realms

If there is one reason to account for this consistency, it is that textile art reflects one perpetuating and unifying theme: that of a pervasive syncretic religious system which appears to have been based upon a reciprocal, implicitly contractual relationship between man and his deities.[10] This was manifested in an iconography whose depictions of deities confirmed and reinforced that relationship, and in a burial ritual conceived to venerate and guarantee that tradition.

This religious content is present from approximately 950 B.C. on, in the earliest textiles with consequential iconographic content: those of the northern highland religious center of Chavin de Huantar and those from the burial sites of the Paracas peninsula, some 170 miles to the south of Lima. It continues right up until the Conquest, in both highland and coastal cultures, and although deities differ considerably according to area and period, the prevalence of a basic metaphysical philosophy is constantly in evidence in textile iconography.

It is thanks to the Spanish chroniclers that we possess recorded evidence to corroborate information that appears on textiles, ceramics, lithic monuments and other archeological sources. The chroniclers tell us about the Incas in considerable detail, and it is clear that this dynamic people conceived of existence as a continuously cyclical relationship among man, gods, the phenomena of nature and the spirits of the departed. There were three realms in their universe: Janan Pacha, the Upper World; Cay Pacha, This World, that is to say, the earth; and Ucu Pacha, the Lower Interior World. Although the gods dwelt in Janan and Cay Pacha, and the spirits, known as *mallqui*, inhabited Ucu Pacha, the three areas were closely linked. For example,

such magical places as craters, rivers and lakes, which were called *pacariscas*, were physically located in This World but originated in the Lower Interior World. Janan and Cay Pacha were symbolically linked through the Inca, the supreme ruler; he was king on earth, but also synonymous with his father, the Sun, and therefore a deity of Janan Pacha.[11]

All this is highly relevant for understanding textile creation and use. Ancient Peru lacked those attributes usually associated with great civilizations: navigable rivers for trade and communication, plentiful arable land, harness animals for human transport or cultivation of the earth, the wheel. The existence of its people—who probably numbered between about eleven and twelve million at the time of the Conquest—was structured upon agriculture, fishing, animal husbandry and weaving.[12] It was agriculture, however, that primarily insured daily subsistence. Thus ancient Andean religion, like the textile art that reflects it, "exalts cosmic forces and the gods of fertility . . . inspired by the primordial urge of the Indian to obtain abundant food, and by the agricultural activity that accomplishes this."[13] It was therefore essential that the main agricultural products— wheat, corn, peppers, potatoes, yucca, etc.—should prosper. All this implied a constant nexus between man, gods, the land and nature.

It was here that the textile process was involved in placating and propitiating those deities capable of insuring the earth's fertility. For the ancient Peruvian, such fertility depended upon combined action by the Upper World, whose gods provided sunlight and rain, and the Lower Interior World, where the *mallqui* spirits could facilitate the growth of plants and crops as well as the creation of river sources.

For the inhabitant of This World, there was thus a tacit obligation to revere the deities of the Upper World and to satisfy the *mallqui* of the Lower Interior World. This is why textile iconography is so frequently a celebration of the omnipotence and omnipresence of deities, and why such care was taken, not only to dress the embalmed bodies of dead dignitaries in sumptuous burial vestments, but also to continue periodic cleaning and maintenance of the funerary bundles after the burial.[14]

Deities appeared in three main forms: as cosmic bodies, phenomena or manifestations of nature; as mythological and epic heroes in divine or human form; and as zoomorphic and fantastic "composite" creatures. There were major and minor deities, as well as ones related to specific areas and activities.[15]

Those related to nature were the Sun, Moon, Thunder, Lightning, the Rainbow, the Pleiades and Venus. Radiant suns, usually with either six or eight rays and made of feathers stitched to a cotton backing, are an especially joyous theme of textile design, and seem to echo the lines of a *jailli*, or sacred poem, in the language that was originally called Runa Simi but given the name Quechua by the Spanish priest Fray Domingo de Santo Tomás. "*Qoyllurpáj Inkan, Inti Yayanchis,*" begins a stanza from the poem *Runa Kamaj* ("O Sun, king of the stars and our father").[16] In the highlands there were various deities associated with thunder and lightning—Illapa, Libiac, Pariacaca and Catequil—

and these appear to have been controlled by Tunupa, one of the several major mythological deities.

Tunupa appears to have been replaced in importance by Viracocha, the foremost Inca deity, whose significance seems to have grown in accordance with Inca expansionism. Viracocha is of special interest, since in the central region of Peru he was considered to be the deity who presided over weaving and embroidery.[17] Whereas Viracocha was essentially a highland god, the major central coast deity was Pachacamac or, to use the original name, Ychma. This god was associated with the great religious shrine located near the mouth of the Lurín valley, some fifteen miles to the south of Lima. When the Incas conquered the area in the mid-fifteenth century, they constructed a temple of the sun and called the site Pachacamac—*pacha* in Quechua meaning "earth," and *camac* being a derivation of the verb "to create." Hence, "creator of the universe," whose existence was accepted by the local priests in exchange for Inca permission to allow continued local veneration of Ychma.[18]

Actually, there does not appear to have been a consensus among the chroniclers with a regard to which specific deity was either supreme or the creator of man. Con, a northern

CHRONOLOGY OF
MAJOR TEXTILE-PRODUCING
CULTURES AND SITES OF PERU
BEFORE THE SPANISH CONQUEST

Approximate Date	NORTH		CENTRAL	SOUTH		
	Coast	Highland	Coast	Coast	Highland	Altiplano
B.C. 1000						
900				PARACAS (Chavin Influence)		
800						
700		CHAVIN DE HUANTAR				
600				PARACAS		
500						
400				NASCA 1 (Proto-Nasca)		
300				& LATE PARACAS		
200	MOCHICA					
100						
0						
A.D. 100						
200						
300						TIAHUANACO
400				NASCA		
500					HUARI	
600						
700						
800	H U A R I E X P A N S I O N					
900	HUARMEY		YCHMA			
1000						
1100	CHIMU		CHANCAY	CHINCHA		
1200	HUARMEY		YCHMA	ICA		
1300					INCA	
1400	I N C A E X P A N S I O N					
1500	PACHACAMAC°					
1532						
	S P A N I S H C O N Q U E S T					

°The name of the Ychma shrine was changed to Pachacamac by the Incas. The names spelled Nasca, Huari and Cuzco in the present book also occur in the literature as Nazca, Wari, Cusco. The names Chavin and Chimu also occur with their Spanish accent as Chavín and Chimú. N.B. Provenience attributions may not always coincide with dates and geographical locations listed in the chronology, since textiles moved around various areas of Peru according to patterns of trade, religious activity and conquest. The extensive time ranges listed for certain textiles (for example, Nasca nonfigurative pieces) occur because their general characteristics remained relatively similar for many centuries, while ceramics found with them reveal wide variations in time.

god with whom Pachacamac had epic struggles, was said first to have created human beings, and then to have transformed them into monkeys and foxes.[19] Together with Naylamp, this deity seems to have dominated a coastal area first controlled by the Mochica, and subsequently by the Chimu peoples.

Three other north coast deities were Cuismancu, Chicopaec and Aiapaec, the latter being frequently shown as a fanged god in Mochica ceramics. Pariacaca was a deity of the central highlands, as was Guari, whose name became synonymous with the culture Huari. And there were gods associated with specific activities. Huamancantac, for example, was the god of guano, while north coast ceramics frequently represent deities associated with wheat and corn—possibly Vichama, god of the day.[20]

These deities appeared in all sorts of forms, and so clear identification of them in textile iconography is very difficult. There simply are not enough specific descriptions. We know that Pariacaca could assume the aspect of lightning, or that Guari was capable of transforming himself into a man, a serpent or the wind. Occasionally the chroniclers give us a clue that is useful in analyzing textile motifs. Sarmiento de Gamboa, for example, in his 1572 *Historia de los Incas*, mentions that Viracocha wore a white robe and carried a staff and book in his hands. But although the reference to the staff is very useful—textile deities constantly carry what may be spears, lances, batons (*bastones*, Sp) or staffs—one has the impression that the author is describing Andean gods in terms of Old Testament imagery. The most reliable reference regarding deities with scepters or *bastones* appears in the one known ancient Quechua manuscript, an anonymous publication entitled *Gods and Men of Huarochiri*, which reportedly dates from around 1598 A.D., and in which the god Pariacaca and his son Tutayquiri use gold *bastones*.[21]

If we exclude the Inca rulers, there do not appear to have been any specific real-life figures of messianic dimensions in ancient Peru, no Christ or Buddha. Nor do we know of any catalytic drama comparable with the Crucifixion, the focal point of so much Western art. The Andean world was not monotheistic, but rather a polytheistic cosmos of pantheistic dimensions. Gods and spirits were everywhere, not only in the phenomena of nature and heroic figures already mentioned, but also in zoomorphic beings—animals, birds, fish, serpents, mammals and, above all, the mystical dragon. Animism was also prevalent, with mountain peaks, stones, volcanic craters and rivers having special meaning.

All this has a great deal to do with textile design. Whereas man was the subject of art in the Middle Ages, and had been, as Kenneth Clark has observed, since the period of Greece and Rome,[22] the themes of ancient Peruvian textiles presuppose a constant divine presence, a cosmos suffused with ineffable manifestations of godly volition.

In 1926 the German anthropologist Ernst Vatter recognized the relevance of this sort of world view. "Today," he wrote, "we begin to doubt our own soulless civilization, and to realize that we have lost what the primitive peoples, despised for so long, possessed to the highest degree: an outlook that includes mankind and the universe within a deeply felt unity."[23] The metaphysical framework of the beliefs and environment of Andean man must therefore constantly be borne in mind as we examine the creation, productivity, types, uses and iconography of pre-Columbian Peruvian textiles.

The Artists and Weavers in Their Historical Setting

Both the artists who created the designs and the weavers who executed them in cloth were anonymous talents whose names and lives are unknown. The high quality of their work is not surprising if we recall the comment of Jean Renoir that masterpieces are made by artisans, not artists. What is, however, so extraordinary is that such a consistently sophisticated creative level was maintained throughout Peru for some two thousand years.

It was also achieved autonomously, that is to say without the benefit of outside influences or continental cultural interchange. And not just in one area. Whether it was in the highlands or along the coast, weaving flourished in a period of unparalleled brilliance. Different styles of weaving, varied interpretations of traditional motifs and distinct uses of color evolved in different areas, rather as schools of painting developed in Renaissance Italy in such centers as Florence, Venice and Rome. But the consistency of aesthetic imagination and technical skill is as pronounced as is the perpetuation of a unifying religious system.

In ancient Peru, these weaving styles are associated with the cultures whose names are derived from the geographical areas where they evolved. The first of these to produce textiles of artistic significance was that of the northern highland religious center of Chavin de Huantar, whose designs on painted cotton may have been made as early as 1000–600 B.C. Their iconography, related to "the jaguar, the large constrictor snake, the cayman, the condor and the eagle," spread to the coast and was initially influential in the south coast Paracas culture, which dates from roughly 1000 B.C. to about 100 B.C.[24]

At this time, the Nasca culture had begun to emerge in the south coast area. After an initial period of transition, referred to as Nasca 1 (Proto-Nasca) and Nasca 2 (Early Nasca), the Nasca people flourished until about 800 A.D.: producing not only magnificent textiles but also highly colored ceramics and the enigmatic "earth drawings" etched into the Nasca plain. On the north coast, from about 400 B.C. until approximately 800 A.D. a culture centered around the Moche river and called Mochica produced prolific quantities of the most realistic and anatomically accurate of all Peruvian ceramics. Unfortunately, the Mochica left behind relatively few textiles, in large part because of the destructive erosion of cloth caused by saltpeter in their area.

By about the seventh century A.D., both Mochica and Nasca textiles were showing the influence of a dynamic, expansionist southern highland people known as Huari. The Huari administrative center was located near present-day Ayacucho, and appears to have developed between approximately 500 and 700 A.D. The Huari people clearly assimilated the religious iconography of what was apparently a very important religious ceremonial center at Tiahuanaco, some 700 miles to the south by road travel. The origins of Tiahuanaco are unclear, as is the reason for its demise, but its inception as a major site may date from about 200–100 B.C. Tiahuanaco, as we shall see later, is very important in terms of textile iconography because of its extremely graphic lithic art.

Toward the eighth or ninth century, a militant and expansionist Huari people appears to have dominated most of the Peruvian coast. Huari textiles have been found in the area of Huarmey, 230 miles north of Lima, and as far south as the Tacna/Arica/Moquegua Chilean border region. Huari influence seems to have been considerable until the decline of the culture toward the eleventh and twelfth centuries. At this time, new regional state cultures sprang up. In the north, around what was probably South America's first great metropolitan area, the adobe city of Chanchan, the Chimu people emerged to continue the traditions of the earlier Mochica. By now Huarmey appears to have become an independent weaving center, with its focus apparently located in the vicinity of the great temple and burial site known as the Castillo. On the central coast, the Chancay valley was evidently a major textile-producing area, with important textiles also coming from the Ancón area, about 30 miles north of Lima, and the Lurín valley and Pachacamac, about 20 miles to the south of Lima. The third regional state culture developed among the seafaring people of Chincha and Ica.

By around 1300 A.D., a dynamic new mountain people, the Incas, was emerging around the southern highland city of Cuzco. However, it was not until the 1430s, when Pacha-cutec ascended to the throne, that the Incas embarked upon their whirlwind territorial expansion. By the mid- to late fifteenth century, they were largely in control of all of Peru, allowing the regional states to maintain a limited degree of self-rule under the overall hegemony of Cuzco. Regional state weaving styles may thus have continued to a great extent, in spite of the simultaneous existence of Inca weaving, right up until the Conquest—and even for a limited period thereafter.

The uncertainty regarding dates is an inevitable consequence of insufficient archeological and historical information. In terms of weaving iconography, it means that the correlation between stylistic and chronological developments cannot be consistently determined. There are also gaps in our knowledge caused by the absence of textiles from certain cultures whose inclement environment perhaps explains why we have no weaving legacy from them: Recuay, Vicus and Lambayeque, for example. Although a few textiles have been excavated in the 13,000-foot-high *altiplano,* and even occasionally in higher locations, the damp weather effectively destroyed most reliable highland data bases for textile dating. Whether buried above ground, in circular stone towers or arch-like tombs called *chullpas,* or below the earth, few survived; and if we possess such representative selections of textiles from the highland peoples of Chavin, Tiahuanaco, Huari and Inca, it is because their Pan-Peruvianism assured their arrival at, and burial in, the desert coast.

What is remarkable about weaving in ancient Peru is that it was done by virtually every social class, even the elite. The Inca ruler himself, as well as the Chosen Women, the Vestal Virgins, wove. As for the great mass of the people, known in Quechua as the *hatunruna,* most male and female members of a typical family were likely to be involved in one of the productive stages that occurred between the collection of the raw materials and the dissemination of the finished article. The chronicler Garcilaso de la Vega tells us: "The women were so accustomed to spinning that they brought their spindles out into the streets or on the highlands when they were on their way to see a friend, and they kept on working after they reached her house, while they were chatting together."[25] Men also did spinning and weaving, especially in special artisan workshops called *cumbicos.*[26] Here highly skilled male weavers called *cumbicamayos* wove luxurious designs with the *cumbi* cloth of the vicuña, that member of the camelid family whose wool was the finest. Were these perhaps the "master weavers" mentioned in the Huarochiri document?[27]

How did the weaving process work? Were assignments farmed out to local households by state-employed middlemen, rather as was done in the early 1600s in rural England? Was the weaving system controlled by the state in earlier cultures, to the degree that it was under the Incas, or did any degree of private enterprise exist? How much initiative, one wonders, could local weavers exercise in the design and composition of textiles, and how much iconography was resolved by state religious or secular authorities? One assumes that institutionalized weaving guilds and workshops did exist; a Mochica ceramic shows weavers working in a group under a supervisor, and the chronicler Xeres, upon arriving in Cajamarca, noted a "great and strong building . . . in which there were many women spinning and weaving cloth for the army of Ataliba [Atahuallpa]."[28]

Since the Incas exacted a textile tribute from their subjects, a generally high weaving standard must have been maintained by the *hatunruna.* However, the finest-quality pieces are unlikely to have been made by the average domestic weaver. The elite classes—the royal family, nobles, the religious and secular hierarchy—monopolized the best textiles, and especially those embellished with feathers or metal.[29] The Indian subjects, on the other hand, were limited to two garments of cotton or wool, as well as a large work cloak, which were issued to them on their wedding day from the state storage deposits. These garments, one for routine use and the other for festivals, had to be employed until they were completely worn out.[30] Additionally, as Padre Cobo tells us, it was expressly forbidden for *hatunruna* to wear lavish or ostentatious textiles.

Materials, Looms, Techniques, Colors

The weavers worked with simple basic materials: wool and cotton. The wool, in natural tones of ivory white, lustrous black, pearly gray and earth tones of sienna, beige and umber, came from the camelid family. The vicuña furnished the wool for the most elite textiles, but it was the fine quality alpaca wool that was best suited for the majority of sophisticated weaving products. As for the wool of the llama, which was often coarse and greasy, it was deemed to be of inferior quality—"abasca," the chronicler Padre Cobo called it.

Wool from the camelid family came from the highlands, but cotton, *Gossypium barbadense,* was grown along the river valleys of the desert coast. It came in five main shades: white (which often assumes a cream-colored patina), tan, brown, dark brown and grayish mauve. It was an "especially durable variety, resistant to both drought and flood and to many kinds of local insect pest."[31] Cloth was embroidered, woven, painted, stamped (with seals dipped into paint), fashioned into delicate net-like gauze pieces and embellished with brilliantly hued feathers and regal gold and silver ornaments. These metal pieces, normally used as thin appliqués, owed their pliability to the annealing process and their frequently embossed designs to the repoussé technique.[32]

Feathers came from the condor, flamingo, owl, guacamayo macaw and parrot species, egret, curassow, tanager, honeycreeper and trogon.[33] Just how feathers were obtained for use in decorative textiles is not clear. The chronicler Guaman Poma de Ayala recounts that boys aged between nine and twelve were responsible for collecting feathers to adorn textiles, but we lack detailed evidence about the feather-gathering process. The Chimu may have kept Muscovy ducks, but there is no evidence that there were organized aviaries like those of pre-Columbian Mexico, where three hundred Indians obtained plumes for the Aztec *amanteca* feather weavers without killing the birds.[34]

In making feather textiles, feathers were generally stitched onto long *hileras* (Sp), or threads, which were then applied to natural, undyed cotton ground. In the case of certain feather masks in the south coast area, feathers were affixed to the cotton surrounding the skull with a paste-like adhesive substance called *masa de maíz* (Sp), made from pulverizing ears of corn into a sort of glue. *Hileras* were generally placed horizontally, but also in a curvilinear pattern, when applying them to cotton textiles.

These ancient Peruvian feather vestments, suffused with sun-drenched color, overlaid with gold and silver ornaments that scintillate with vivid radiance or quiver with lambent flickerings—is there anything as sumptuous, as regal and as sensual in the art of the Americas? Perhaps the exotic headdresses of pre-Columbian Mexico, the spectacular regalia of D. H. Lawrence's Plumed Serpent: the demiurgic Quetzalcóatl, the Toltec priest-god with human or rattlesnake body who was called Kukulcán by the Mayas.[35] In North American Indian society, feathers have habitually been associated with prowess, stature and shamanism: the imperious Mandan war bonnets of eagle feathers, often enriched with curved buffalo horns, or the feather-bedecked masks of the Kachinas, doll-like Hopi dancers who incarnated the spirits of the departed.[36] When Atahuallpa went to meet Pizarro, Xeres recounts that his open palanquin revealed sides "lined with plumes of macaws, of many colors, and adorned with plaques of gold

and silver." Here was resplendent plumage for these great leaders of a bygone era, whose heads, in the words of the famed Nicaraguan poet Rubén Darío, "were encircled with plumes of great value."[37]

There is a transcendental aura about these feather textiles. Explosions of iridescent hues, multitiered surfaces ranging from velvet-sheen smoothness to scumbled, wind-blown coruscation—what we have here are extraordinary art objects, endowed with visual opulence and recondite mysticism. Their implicit three-dimensionality is enhanced both by the assemblage technique of appliqué and by collage, as in the case of south coast Nasca and Huari funerary feather masks.

Feathers were considered to possess magical qualities, and were used by *mosoc* and *runatingui*—types of shamans and soothsayers—to overcome enemies in such rites as the *cuscoviza,* to inspire and foretell amorous conquests, and to caress the face of the Inca ruler.[38] They were also an indispensable element in dances and fiestas, which in the ancient Andean world had an especially sacred significance. In the *chocano,* for example, a sling match between the youth of Upper and Lower Cuzco, the dancers were "dressed in black tunics ending in a white border, further adorned with white feathers."[39]

The Spanish authorities were so apprehensive about the magical attributes of feathers that Bishop de la Peña Montenegro, in listing remedies to destroy idolatry and uproot superstitions and witchcraft, prohibited dances on the grounds that such items as feather plumage were used, and were "instruments of evil."[40]

All these extraordinary Peruvian textiles were made with the most basic elements. The looms used for weaving were rudimentary, and the Spaniards were amazed that anyone could accomplish such fine work with equipment "so small and cheap," according to Padre Cobo, "that with two sticks as thick as one's arm, the loom is ready." Actually, three types of looms were used: the backstrap loom, a horizontal ground loom whose four corners were stabilized by four vertical sticks, and a special vertical type that was apparently used for producing high-quality *cumbi* cloth.

The vertical loom, an apparent innovation of the highland Huari people, enabled the construction of tapestry panels of hitherto unknown dimensions—some 22 inches in width and about 80 inches in length. As Alan Sawyer, former director of the Washington, D. C., Textile Museum, has pointed out, woven pieces of such dimensions did not reach the coast until the period of Tiahuanaco–Huari expansion. Two of these panels sewn together, with a slit left open in the middle to accommodate passage of the head, compose the classic, almost square Huari sleeveless tapestry shirts that represent some of the greatest technical and artistic weaving ever done in the world.[41]

Weaving techniques developed from what Edouard Versteylen, curator of textiles at the Peruvian National Museum of Anthropology and Archeology in Lima, has called a "rudimentary first stage: that of netting and twining, whereby two separate elements, the warp (length) and the weft (width), were used to construct the fabric." The major excavations carried out by Junius Bird at Huaca Prieta in the north coast Chicama valley area revealed that cotton fabrics of twined construction from the pre-ceramic period made their appearance between roughly 3000 B.C. and 2000 B.C. Warp patterning was also used. "Thus," Versteylen goes on, "even before the invention of the loom, requisite to weaving, Peruvians were expert in other manufacturing methods such as twining, looping, coiling, knotting, matting and basketry. With the perfection of the loom and the subsequent use of heddles to guide the warp threads, all techniques were being employed in the last centuries before Christ."[42]

It was during the Early Horizon (ca. 1400–400 B.C.), as Ann P. Rowe has indicated, that the use of all textile techniques subsequently employed in pre-Columbian Peru seems to have been established.[43] At this time, Jane P. Dwyer comments, "the most common designs were being created structurally in patterned weaves, double and triple cloth, brocading and gauze, as well as in non-loom techniques such as twining, braiding, knotting, sprang and looping." Embroidery, destined to account for many of the greatest Paracas textiles, was still relatively little used, cotton was more commonly employed than wool and the range of color was still relatively limited.[44] By this time painted plain cloth and tapestry were also in evidence.

The Early Intermediate Period (ca. 400 B.C.–500 A.D.) ushered in more extensive and variegated colors, which were used to create some of the most mysterious and fantastic compositions encountered in ancient Peruvian weaving. Textiles from the first two epochs of the Early Intermediate Period come largely from the Paracas peninsula, but in reality constitute a transitional phase into the neighboring Nasca culture; they belong to Nasca 1, or the Proto-Nasca period, from about 500 B.C. to 200 B.C. and to the overlapping Nasca 2, or Early Nasca period, with approximate dates of 300 B.C. to 200 B.C.

It is at this time that colors of spectacular richness and tonal variety are first used. Indeed, upon first seeing these startling geranium lakes, delicate violets and mauves, iridescent turquoise blues, exhilarating lemon yellows and brilliant magentas, one's impression is of a Mediterranean painting by Pierre Bonnard or Henri Matisse rather than of an ancient textile. We do not know how institutionalized the process of dyeing was in these early years, but in the later Andean *tullpuni* system, the *tanticamayoc* dyers "used plants to obtain all existing colors, often with numerous variations."[45] Mary Elizabeth King, former Curator of Western Hemisphere Textiles in the Textile Museum, Washington, D. C., has noted:

Dyes could be combined to produce an almost unlimited number of shades. Red came from a plant related to madder, Relbunium, or from cochineal made from the insect, coccus cacti. Blue was obtained from indigo. Yellow could have been made from a number of plants. Purple was sometimes obtained from a mollusc [I have found these still scattered along the coastline of the Paracas peninsula—J.W.R.], as was the famous Tyrian purple. Little is known about the mordants involved in dyeing, but analysis has shown that both alum and iron were used for this purpose. From archeological evidence we know that cotton was occasionally dyed with the seeds attached; wool was probably dyed before spinning, though probably less frequently.

Yarn dyeing, however, was undoubtedly the most common dyeing method.[46]

Technical characteristics can be extremely useful in identifying textiles by area and culture. As Ann P. Rowe has indicated in her comprehensive *Warp-Patterned Weaves of the Andes*, a highland origin for a textile found on the coast can be inferred if the material is entirely alpaca yarn—the most important source of material for the production of textiles. Secondly, certain cultures created types of textiles with technical attributes and characteristics peculiar to them: Huari pile hats, for example, or Chancay net-like gauzes. Thirdly, certain weaving characteristics used by a specific people can provide invaluable data regarding provenance; for example, the use of paired warps and single wefts, S-spinning and single-ply yarns permits the identification of a textile as Chimu even though it was excavated on the central or south coasts of Peru.[47]

The tightness and fineness of ancient Peruvian weaving is legendary, its meticulous precision and attention to detail suggesting that much of the best weaving may have been done by relatively young people. Would older weavers, for example, have possessed the eyesight to achieve the 398 threads in the Chincha-Ica textile fragment in the Rafael Larco Herrera museum?—a statistical figure, Larco suggests, "which has never previously been achieved and has never been equalled since."[48]

Textile Objects and Their Uses

Cloth was used to make an extensive variety of functional, ceremonial and religious objects: weighing scales, shoes, boxes, sails, pillows, breastplates, cushions, masks, tents, bed covers, door hangings, slings, three-dimensional decorative items like birds and trees, and several types of bags: *chuspas* (small purses), *wall'kepus* (larger bags) and *costales* (saddle bags, Sp). It was, however, garments and wrapping cloths that were the textile items produced in the greatest quantities.

It is rare to think of clothing as great art, and there really is not anything in history comparable in this sense with ancient Peruvian textiles. It is the garments and mantles that provide the most rewarding aesthetic experience, perhaps because their relatively large size and square or rectangular formats most closely approximate a traditional painting. Even though not made to be hung as wall adornments, many work very effectively in this way.

These vestments are known by an eclectic and often confusing miscellany of names that are either English, Spanish or Quechua. For example, what we call a shirt, sleeveless tunic or tabard in English was a *cushma* in Quechua and a *poncho* in Spanish. Like the *unku*, a shirt with sleeves, it was normally worn by men, and covered with a sort of cape called a *yacolla*. The *huara*, a type of trousers of normally undecorated plain cloth, completed the man's basic dress.

A woman's normal garment was the *anacu*, a long tunic that might be covered with a shawl called *llikla* or *awayo*.[49]

There were numerous accessories. *Llautus, turbantes*

(Sp), *vinchas* and *borlas* (Sp) were headbands worn across the forehead. Headpieces included *gorras* (hats, Sp) and *cascos* (helmets, Sp), the latter often being made of reeds or cane strips joined together and covered with cloth, as well as *coronas* (crowns, Sp) and *máscaras* (masks, Sp), both of which were frequently adorned with meticulously applied feathers. *Pecheras* (breastplates, Sp) and *collares* (collars, Sp) were also made of decorated cloth, as were *taparrabos* (Sp), loincloths normally configured in a triangular dimension. Sashes and belts apparently used by both men and women were *chumpis* and *fajas* (Sp).

The final category, that of the mantle or wrapping cloth, included the smallish square or rectangular pieces known as *esclavinas* (Sp) or *nañacas* and the large textile mantle called *manto* (Sp). Their size varies, but generally averages about five or six feet in length and width; those of Paracas tend traditionally to be larger, and some of the north coast painted wrapping shrouds attain lengths of twenty feet, and occasionally far more.[50]

The role of the textile in the Inca state has been aptly summarized by John V. Murra, the first author to examine in detail its multifaceted functions in pre-Conquest Andean society:

> A primary source of state revenues, an annual chore among peasant obligations, a common sacrificial offering, cloth could also serve at different times and occasions as a status symbol or a token of enforced citizenship, as burial furniture, bride-wealth, or armistice-sealer. No political, military, social or religious event was complete without textiles being volunteered or bestowed, burned, exchanged or sacrificed.[51]

Previous cultures probably attributed some degree of similar importance to some or all of the activities mentioned by Murra, for religious and social customs, and ceremonies associated with them, have traditionally changed little in the conservative Andean Indian world. Additionally, as Jane P. Dwyer notes, "archeological evidence is now accumulating to indicate that cloth may have had many similar functions in earlier Peruvian cultures as well."[52]

Although preceding cultures may have not been as theocratic as was the Inca state, it is probable that religious influence was paramount in all Andean peoples of ancient Peru, and constantly reflected in their art. The recognition that the deities needed to be eulogized and placated is manifest throughout Peruvian weaving, a fact that would suggest that religious uses of the textile were the predominant ones.

The role of the textile in the religious sphere was to dress and adorn deities like Ychma, to serve as a sacrificial object, to clothe people destined for sacrifices, to enhance the burial ritual, to invoke magical powers, to enrich ceremonies, festivals and sacred dances held in honor of such special events as the harvest or the Inca's birthday, and to cover temple doors facing east.[53]

The textile was involved, Garcilaso de la Vega tells us, in "almost every principal sacrifice," being hurled into ravines or burned in great pyres as a cathartic propitiation to the gods. An example of its use to clothe sacrificial victims is the *capocha*, a ceremony held to honor the accession to power of each new Inca or to celebrate the capture of Huascar by his brother Atahuallpa during the internecine struggle for power between the two brothers which followed the death of their father Huayna Capac in 1537 A.D.[54] A shirt clothing an infant, one of a group found in a Chimu grave and shown in Illus. 76, may have been used in such a ceremony.

One reason that the textile was the most prized object in ancient Peru was that it was believed to possess magical/mystical attributes derived from its proximity to the human body. Used clothing of the Inca ruler or of prominent dignitaries had a certain talismanic significance, as did textiles whose association with funerary bundles brought them into contact with *mallqui*. The funerary bundle consisted of the body of a male or female dignitary in either a supine or fetal position wrapped and covered with textiles of varying types, quantities and quality. Once buried in a *huaca*, or holy place, the deceased was considered to have become a *mallqui* spirit.

Textiles were involved in numerous magical rites. *Chuspa* purses were used by *socyocs* (shamans) to carry *chumpirun*, small pebbles for foretelling the future. *Mosocs* (soothsayers) obtained inspiration for their prophecies by sleeping on bags, slings or mantles if their client was male, and on *chumpi* belts when female.[55] Judicious use of textiles, it was thought, could cause irrevocable damage to one's enemies. For example, inducing an adversary to step on a thread plied in black and white yarn, or hanging an effigy figure dressed in the captured garments of an opponent, were acts believed capable of causing death.[56] Finally, textiles and their accessories played a role in manifestations designed to stimulate psychological support against the enemy; in the *cuscoviza* rite, shamans danced around a fire into which the feathers of the *quico* bird were thrown, and shouted "Ussachu (let us conquer)!"[57]

For all these reasons, the textile was treated with consummate care and respect. While being woven, it was anointed with *sancu*, a toasted flour mixed with hot water, to give it durability and protect its wearer from illness. After burial, textiles were periodically cleaned; the *p'acha t'aksay*, for example, was a ceremonial washing within eight days of burial designed to prevent the dead from returning to haunt the living.[58] The fear that this might occur was a very real one. "For ancient man," writes the Peruvian historian Santisteban, "death was the result of a magical action brought against him."[59] Thus the fate that had befallen them could antagonize the *mallqui* and provoke their vengeance against the living. Hence the indispensability of the burial ritual as a preemptive act of propitiation.

Thus not only the funerary bundle, but also the accompanying feather, stone, ceramic and metal objects—garments, fans, baskets, bags, jewelry, slings, mirrors and clothing accessories, in short all the lares and penates of an aristocratic household—were destined to insure the departed *mallqui* spirits a harmonious last voyage to, and comfortable resting place in, the Lower Interior World. "A people that respects the cult of the dead will always take great care with the burial ritual," wrote the French explorer Charles Wiener during his archeological excavations near Ancón on the central coast of Peru in 1876.[60] As we shall now see, the textile was equally respected in a variety of ways in daily life in ancient Peru.

The Role of Textiles in Social Mores

The textile was inextricably and inexorably involved in major rites and functions of social life. Garments were given as presents to celebrate a youth's formal admission into society at the time of his first haircut and the *warachikuy* rite.[61] Cristóbal de Molina tells us that such garments, which the candidate changed at each phase of the ceremony, were tied to traditions according to the design, color and type of textile used, and reinforced the ties of parenthood. The chronicler Murúa further indicates that textiles were institutionalized marriage gifts.[62]

The Inca state fully recognized the usefulness of the textile as a political instrument of power. A gift to distinguished visitors to the Inca capital of Cuzco "always included textiles" as a symbol of esteem and respect. The textile was used to reward compliant vassals and meritorious subordinates, to placate mutiny-prone soldiers and to bribe and coerce recalcitrant adversaries.[63] The chronicler Cabello de Valboa describes how the Spaniards, desperate to quell the post-Conquest guerrilla resistance in the Vilcabamba area, offered the tenacious chief Sayri Thupi textiles as a lure to cease hostilities. Even Atahuallpa, albeit unsuccessfully, dispatched a present of textiles to his half-brother Huascar as an inducement to end their fratricidal strife.[64]

The bestowing of textiles as gifts in Inca society was a distinct honor, both for the donor who could afford such largesse and for the recipient deemed sufficiently worthy. In the epic Quechua drama *Ollantay*, when the resentful chamberlain of the rebel general Pikichaki is asked what he wants to mollify him, the answer is immediate: "Garments, to give as gifts to people."[65] Such gifts may have connoted the implicit initiation of reciprocal obligations, Murra suggests, or even of formal dependency. Taking textiles away from bureaucrats who were delinquent in their work, the chroniclers tell us, was also used as punishment.[66]

State bureaucracy used one particular textile item—the *quipus*—to fulfill a vital role in organizational planning, control and recording of statistical data. The *quipus* was a mnemonic device made of threads. There was one main horizontal thread, from which hung differently colored ones with knots at specific points tied to indicate quantities of population, food supplies, food strengths and similar information of importance. The Spaniards considered the *quipus* to be fatidic elements of idolatry which inspired witchcraft and magic, and resorted to continual institutional measures to have them destroyed.[67]

The *quipus* is a practical rather than artistic object, but it does have lyrical implications, as an old Quechua poem suggests: "I wanted a llama/with a golden coat,/bright as the sun/strong as love/soft as clouds,/unravelled by dawn,/in order to make/a knotted rope/for keeping track/of moons that pass,/of flowers that die."[68]

The Incas used information stored on *quipus* for tax assessments, production quotas and contingency planning—to calculate food allocations per area in event of shortages, for example. Their administrative system was meticulously organized, and steps were taken to insure it was not disrupted; thus, population movements were not allowed unless specifically authorized by the state. Here again the textile was indispensable: it functioned as a sort of identity card, since subjects were obliged at all times to wear an identifiable object of clothing. The southern highland Collas wore a woolen type of cap, for example, while the chronicler José de Acosta narrates that it was an "inviolable law" that every individual wear at all times the *vincha*, or headband, of his particular area.[69]

Such a headband was used by the Inca ruler himself as a sign of sovereignty. Pedro Pizarro describes it as the *llautu*, and Xeres tells us that Atahuallpa had a *borla* which was a "woolen fringe across the forehead, crimson in color, of a silk-like aspect and fastened to the head by cords."[70] Textiles symbolized rank, prestige and professional occupation—but not only in the case of royalty and the elite. Staff functionaries, soldiers and other professional classes probably had distinctive attire. The thousand men with lances who constituted Atahuallpa's advance guard in Cajamarca wore a livery of "white and red squares, like a chessboard," and the Parianas, a sort of organized agricultural police in the Inca period, carried *bastones* decorated with characteristic textile tassels.[71]

The state evidently used immense quantities of textiles for daily functional purposes, burial and sacrificial rites and military requirements. The chronicler Estete remarks that enormous supplies of textiles at Atahuallpa's camp in Cajamarca were to be allocated to recruits on their first day of induction; such textiles were probably kept in the type of storehouses that the Spaniards frequently encountered, and which elicited from Pedro Pizarro the incredulous observation that he could not believe that so many such storehouses existed.[72] The chronicler Agustín de Zarate states that in some cases sufficient textiles were stored in *tambos*, rest and ceremonial centers, to supply as many as twenty or thirty thousand troops.

If the state constantly required large supplies of textiles, it necessarily had to insure the production of sufficient raw materials to accommodate the needs of the weavers. On the coast, where the basis for weaving was cotton, it has been estimated that the approximate amount of this material required for only one Paracas funerary bundle was about three hundred square meters, the output of more than one hectare.[73] The main burial site of Paracas, the famed necropolis of Wari Kayan that lies astride the Cerro Colorado hill on the Paracas peninsula, yielded 429 funerary bundles during the October 1927 excavations that followed Julio C. Tello's extraordinary initial discovery in 1925. There were men, women and children, dignitaries of the priestly and aristocratic classes, and their heads had in many cases been subjected to trepanning or vertical deformation.[74] Their embalmed bodies were often wrapped in many mantles, and this discovery was repeated countless times—not only in the *necrópolis*-type flat-earth cemeteries or in the funnel-like Paracas *cavernas*-type cave tombs, but also in numerous other burial areas of other cultures scattered along the coast.

How did the state obtain its raw materials, the cotton from the coast, and the wool from the camelid family in the highlands? And what systems existed to coordinate the obtaining and application of accessory adornments—gold, silver and feathers?

During the Inca period, such basic resources as land and animals were in effect owned by either the federal government or by local authorities, with the usufruct of certain pieces of terrain being granted to members of the state for specific periods of time.[75] It is probable that the masses—the *hatunruna*—furnished the materials for the modest textile garments destined for their own use, but that the wool, cotton, feathers and metal adornments required to make the spectacular pieces were provided by federal or local authorities. Certainly these authorities exacted a textile tribute or quota, which was known as the textile *mita;* this was enforced both by inspection and by the meting out of punishments for those who failed to comply with their weaving obligations.[76] Exactly what these obligations were is not clear. The chronicler Cieza de León reported that each household had to provide annually one mantle, as well as one shirt per family member, to the authorities. Other chroniclers indicate that there were no limits as to what might be required, but the authors do not specify if they are referring to tribute to local *curacas* (chiefs) or to the central government in Cuzco.[77]

We know very little about economic systems and trade patterns in ancient Peru, but it is logical to assume that textiles were an important item of barter. The chronicler Inigo Ortiz does mention several market exchanges—dried llama meat (*charqui*) and potatoes in exchange for cotton, for example, but insufficient information exists to establish any sort of a coherent economic pattern.[78] Probably the most illuminating report on this subject is one that provides evidence of textiles being used for trade outside of Peru. It deals with Lt. Bartolomé Ruiz, of Moguer, the pilot during Francisco Pizarro's second expedition to Peru in late 1526/early 1527. Ruiz met a raft sailing north under cotton sails, with a cargo that contained "many wool and cotton mantles and Moorish-type tunics . . . and other pieces of clothing colored with cochineal, crimson, blue, yellow and all other colors, and worked with different types of ornate embroidery, in figures of birds, animals, fishes and trees . . . they were taking all this to trade for fish shells, from which they make counters . . . ."[79]

In view of their value, textiles were protected with inordinate care. Both Quizquiz and Ruminawi, Inca generals who opposed the Spaniards, destroyed storehouses full of textiles to prevent them from falling into Spanish hands. Thus Ruminawi, knowing of the approach of the Spanish commander Benalcázar, burned "a storeroom of very rich clothing which had been kept there since the time of Huayna Capac."[80] Atahuallpa himself demonstrated his preoccupation for his textile assets when he chided the Spanish priest Father Vicente because the Spaniards had robbed textiles from his storehouses en route from the coast to Cajamarca.[81]

The significance attributed to the textile as an object meant that, inevitably, special attention would be dedicated to the iconography: subject matter and compositions. This theme is of cardinal significance, for it is the iconography that has assured the ancient Peruvian textile its merited place in world art.

PART II: **ICONOGRAPHY**

Categories and General Characteristics

A textile iconography structured around the synergistic relationship linking the human, zoomorphic, inanimate and divine worlds must have seemed very little like art to Spaniards reared in a country that, shortly after the conquest of Peru in 1532, was to produce such painters as Velázquez, El Greco, Murillo and Zurbarán. Certain textiles may have seemed familiar to them: the brilliantly colored, boldly designed south coast nonfigurative pieces, for example. Some of these clearly resemble heraldic emblems, coats of arms, flags, banners and pennants. If a responsive visual chord was struck, it would have been at this level, rather than at the aesthetic one.

Traditional views of what constitutes art have changed radically in the last hundred years, however, and as we look at the multifaceted iconography of ancient Peruvian textiles it is useful to bear in mind the prescient vision of the French Symbolist environment of Maurice Denis in the late nineteenth century:

A painting, before being a picture of a nude woman, a horse or an event, is essentially a plane surface covered with colors organized in a certain order . . . the artist must carry out a reasoned stylization; he must use in his work only lines, forms and specific colors which succeed unequivocally in establishing his particular goal; he must exaggerate, attenuate and distort, not only according to his personal vision, but also according to the needs of the idea to be expressed.[82]

The remarkable applicability of these ideas to pre-Columbian Peruvian textile design will be evident as we examine Andean iconography.

All ancient Peruvian textile iconography is of three basic categories: (1) figurative motifs, either of realistic and recognizable or else of fantastic themes; (2) symbolic themes composed of pictographs and ideograms; (3) nonfigurative and abstract compositions. Although some or all of these three categories of subject matter are found in most of the cultures, they do not necessarily occur with the same consistency in each. For example, figurative themes dominate Paracas, Chimu and Chancay textiles, while ideographic symbols characterize Tiahuanaco, Huari and Inca weaving. As for nonfigurative compositions, they are primarily found in south coast Nasca, Huari and Ica designs.

What we do find is a series of general design characteristics that prevail regularly throughout two millennia of Andean weaving, and constitute a modular framework for textile iconography.

The first point to note is that, although textiles were made most commonly to be used as a vestment or wrapping cloth, their rectangular and square formats suggest the pictorial surface and dimensions of a painting. It is just that they are made of cloth rather than canvas.

The second point that strikes one is the subject matter, which is far more limited than that used by the ceramicists, especially those of Nasca, Chimu and Mochica. Ceramics reveal an eclectic and prolific range of themes: still life, genre, portraiture, sexual mores, illnesses and infirmities, punishments, household tasks, commercial transactions, animal and vegetable life, dramas of war and conquest, fishing and agriculture activities, manifestations of divine volition, the cyclical pattern of birth, adolescence, maturity, old age and death, and so on. Textile subjects are far less varied. Anecdotal scenes—of war, fishing, worship, etc.— do occur, but the major effort is devoted to the representation of deities in the form of anthropomorphic, zoomorphic or "composite" beings, or of celestial bodies, and to the portrayal of human subjects either wearing masks or functioning as "god impersonators."

Composite beings are those that combine human, divine, animal and other characteristics: a human body with an avian head, for example. The concept of metamorphosis, passage and transference is prevalent, just as in the anonymous late sixteenth-century Quechua *Huarochiri* manuscript, in which gods are constantly transformed into humans, animals, birds, inanimate objects (like a rock) or elements related to nature, such as the winds. In the textiles of Paracas and Nasca 2 (Early Nasca), where one finds the most complex and fantastic composite beings in all ancient Peruvian textile iconography, human ears may become flowers and tongues are likely to be transposed into serpents or centipedes. Such composite figures often assume the enigmatic, and even horrific, attributes frequently associated with mythological figures.

Static postures are more frequent than dynamic ones, although a sense of physical movement is found, especially in painted textiles of the type in Illus. 41, where a definite feeling of motion is apparent. The more static motifs are often brought to life by lively expressions, which imbue them with a certain spontaneity and psychological animation.

Character and individualism, however, are not human facets with which the ancient Peruvian artist is particularly concerned. Motifs tend to be rendered more as graphic realizations than as specific personalities, so that although faces do show expression—whimsical, smiling, even ferocious miens—they tend generally to be noncommittal and objective. Certainly there is an absence, at least to our eyes, of subtle emotional nuances. Sentimentality of any type— compassion, sensitivity, tenderness, love, introspection— does not really seem to interest the weaver.

Nor do we find much interaction, physical or psychological, between the subjects in large compositions. Almost totally lacking is that sense of communication that we have come to expect from thousands of years of Western art: the sort of philosophical tension, for example, that a Masaccio fresco establishes between secondary figures in the composition and the central personage—a central, focal personage which Baroque art would deliberately highlight through dramatic effects of drawing or light.

This central figure in much of Western art since roughly the time of Giotto, and then the Quattrocento period, was likely to be either the Virgin and Child, God, Christ or the Trinity. And since the birth, life, crucifixion and resurrection of Christ was the catalytic drama of Christianity, this cycle came to be the leitmotiv of a great deal of artistic expression in the Western world for more than 600 years. In the Andean environment, however, there was neither one comparable messianic figure, nor one central spiritual drama, to serve as focal points for graphic composition.

Perhaps this is one reason why we find no apparent concern in ancient Peruvian textiles with such chronological and environmental factors as place, season, weather, date and time, those anecdotal details which relate so much Mediterranean art to specific biblical, historical and other events.

Nor is any attempt made to render light, shadow, effects of rain, storms and lightning, in the traditional sense. Certainly these ephemeral, fugitive manifestations of nature's omnipotence and splendor impressed themselves indelibly upon the soul of ancient Andean man; but he found different ways to portray them. There are none of those storm-lashed seas of Turner, none of the great cumulus-packed skies of Jacob van Ruysdael, none of the glowing sunrises of Monet. Instead, we get glorious renditions of the deities that created them: celestial suns that are lyrically painted or aglow with multihued feathers, mystical renditions of the moon goddess Si or dramatic depictions of the two-headed dragon or serpent symbolizing tempests and rain. The deities themselves, rather than their existential actions, are the graphic themes of the textile artist.

Design surfaces tend to be flat and two-dimensional, rather like Egyptian frescos—but in style, rather than in content: whereas the ancient artists of the Nile valley celebrated the beauty of woman, female pulchritude as we know it is of no concern to pre-Conquest Peruvian weavers. Modeling to create volume is nonexistent in their work, and the traditional concept of space, with emphasis upon perspective, depth, a horizon and vanishing point, generally either eluded them, or else did not matter to them.

There are certain exceptions that suggest at least an awareness of three-dimensional space. This was sometimes implied by specific design conventions, as occurs in certain Nasca 2 (Early Nasca) compositions. As Jane P. Dwyer has clarified, hands are shown actually grasping objects, in notable contrast with their rendition in textiles of Proto-Nasca (Nasca 1) or Paracas 10 (the last epoch of the Early Horizon), where they merely lie across the supposedly held object.[83] A second exception is the way in which unconventional treatment of form and perspective sometimes creates an intellectual, or visual, sense of depth, rather than that imposed by conventional perspective and anatomy. For example, stark linear delineation of a certain part of the body may cause that element to "jump out" at the viewer, as often occurs with Huari textile design.

A third area in which a feeling of space is apparent is in nonfigurative and abstract compositions. Here, rather as in twentieth-century art, "the sensation of space is brought about by color dynamics alone."[84] As an example, in the Nasca mantle of multicolored rectangles shown in Illus. 60, a midnight blue suggests recessional space when juxtaposed with old-gold yellow.

One corollary effect of the flat surface, and one that is visually very exciting, is the immediacy or "close-up" effect created by large images that seem to loom out of the picture plane. Not only is their monumental aspect aesthetically stimulating; it also serves to confront the viewer with a psychological fait accompli, forcing one to take unequivocal notice of the contours, shape and form of the object depicted. Illus. 16, 17, 27 and 28 are excellent illustrations of this sort of monumental image.

Distortion and fragmentation of motifs, as well as a tendency to cut off or abruptly crop compositions—the latter feature being one that did not really affect Western art until Japanese prints reached Paris in the second half of the nineteenth century—are characteristic. These tendencies are not surprising in the twentieth century, but evidence has not reached us of artists in other continents resorting to these imaginative conventions with the same creativity that Peruvian weavers used.

Although many of these compositions are highly complex, and involve a multiplicity of shapes and forms of all sizes, a noteworthy symmetry is almost always present. Order, harmony and logic invariably assert themselves. This graphic discipline is enhanced by the deliberate use of previously mentioned design conventions: allover compositions, in which a central focal point is excluded and all areas of the graphic surface enjoy equal importance, and serial imagery, in which "identical forms are repeated throughout the length and breadth of a composition, so that they are completely interchangeable and can be read up and down, diagonally or back and forth in any direction."[85]

Often, images seem to reflect the philosophic concept of dualism, which Luis Valcarcel and María Rostworowski de Diez Canseco have analyzed in terms of the Inca period. We do not know much about dualism in the pre-Inca period, but certainly several of its graphic ramifications are pervasive presences in earlier textile iconography. In the Nasca sleeveless shirts in Illus. 10 and 11, for example, two "mirror images" similar in size and shape, but differing in color, confront one another from opposite spaces. Dualism was a constant factor in Inca life—military units had two commanders, towns had two sections (Upper and Lower Cuzco, for example) and gods had dual personalities: a heroic and dark side, in the case of Pachacamac. The philosophic concepts of dualism are symbolized by the words *yanantin* and *yanapaque*, which refer generally to bodily symmetry, mirror imagery and to the alter ego, helper or shadow of the primary figure.[86]

Ancient Peruvian textile imagery is replete with the dual motif. Sometimes heads occur within heads, as can be noted in Illus. 3, where bewhiskered feline visages are superimposed upon foreheads of primary figures. In Huari textiles, one body may contain two heads in profile, facing inward toward each other in such a way that they simultaneously confront the viewer as one frontal face—a *trompe-l'œil* effect of the type that one encounters in a Juan Gris Cubist painting. An excellent example is shown in Illus. 53.

"Interlocking" design formats are probably the most common manifestation of graphic dualism. They consist of one body with heads at each end (as opposed to the single body with bicephalic attributes, which is also found). These heads may be identical or, when read right way up and then upside down, turn out to be very different. Interlocking themes occur frequently in Chimu and Chancay textiles especially, and favor heads of birds, serpents, felines and deity figures often joined by little more than a brief diagonal or curvilinear line to suggest the body.

The treatment of subject matter, from its basic realistic format through stylistic processes of simplification, stylization and geometricization, occurs in the three general categories of figurative, symbolic and nonfigurative/abstract iconography which will now be examined.

Figurative Motifs

Themes portrayed vary considerably in recognizability, since some are realistic representations and others fantastic, mythological "composite" beings that conform to no specific identifiable criterion.

The majority of figurative motifs are human or zoomorphic. However, although they are generally delineated with clarity, their identity, origin and meaning are often quite unclear. We need constantly to bear in mind that the ancient Peruvian world was one rich in imaginative metaphor and symbolism—the chief Tantañamca is mentioned in the *Huarochiri* manuscript as possessing yellow, red and blue llamas, for example. Like the Celts, the Andean peoples were strongly conscious of "in-between" states, as a Quechua poem illustrates: "In the morning/drops of dew/on the flowers/are tears the moon/wept all night."[87]

Anthropomorphic Motifs. It is very often not clear if human motifs are mortals venerating deities, in acts of worship, festivals and processions, whether they are actually gods in anthropomorphic form or whether they are "god impersonators." The position of outstretched arms, for example, which is so common in textile iconography, suggests both invocation and benediction. Is it possible, given the notions of dualism and the cosmic totality with which these ancient peoples viewed the universe, that such figures were aimed at expressing the concept of synergistic ties between gods and mortals, rather than specific individuals per se? If individual deities were indeed the motifs, then presumably such major gods as Viracocha, Pariacaca, Guari, Pachacamac, Con, Naylamp, et al., would be represented on textiles produced by cultures that particularly venerated them.

Anthropomorphic motifs occur mainly as frontal or profile figures, which are either full-length or, as in certain north coast pieces, truncated at the waist. There are two great religious sites whose lithic iconography suggests a graphic source: Tiahuanaco and Chavin de Huantar, which share such common characteristics as frontal deities and a feline cult.

The most significant monument at Tiahuanaco is a stone arch, roughly four meters wide by three meters high, with a frieze of sculpted stone stretching across the top third of the structure. Its name, the Gateway of the Sun, is somewhat arbitrary, even though the large central frontal figure does have rays emanating from his head. Tears in the form of stylized jaguars drop from his eyes, his outstretched arms grasp what appears to be a scepter or *bastón,* and his legs are firmly and symmetrically planted atop a steplike dais. This figure is flanked on each side by 24 personages, eight in each row, that are considerably smaller; they are winged and depicted in a running stance, as though they were *chasqui* couriers or messengers. The top and bottom rows are human figures, while those in the center have heads that may be masks or actual heads of condors. Everything about these figures on the Gateway—their posture, facial characteristics, accoutrements—is echoed in not only the highland weaving of Tiahuanaco and Huari, but also in such major coastal textile sites as Huarmey. This stone relief, wrote the noted German archeologist Max Uhle, "synthesizes the most important ideas of the religious faith of Tiahuanaco."[88]

The stone visages of Tiahuanaco are serene, almost benign. Those of Chavin, on the other hand, are more complex, more zoomorphic and more ferocious in expression.

Although anthropomorphic figures are largely depicted in a fixed, static immobility, they are also shown flying through the air, fighting, leading llamas, aboard totora-reed fishing craft called *caballitos* (Sp), participating in sacred dances, processions and festivals, and occasionally in other day-to-day activities. But the main focus for figures-in-movement is on events related to war. The most eloquent reminder that these were warlike people occurs not in textile iconography, but in the incised blocks of stone comprising the 400-foot-long stone facade of the temple of Sechín, near Casma and about 240 miles north of Lima. Some of the figures have a definite Mayan quality to them; certainly their aspect is terrifying, for they use their sharply filed fingernails to gouge out their victims' eyes, tongues and entrails. It is as poignant a testimony to the brutal triumph of the victors, and the anguish of the vanquished, as is Picasso's painting of Guernica.

So it is not surprising that textile designs reflect this bellicose spirit. Warriors brandish lances or half-moon-shaped *tumi* knives while they pull their adversaries' hair, guard fortresses and sacred places, and hunt trophy heads. An ancient Quechua poem captures the mood: "We shall drink from the skull of the traitor/We shall wear his teeth as a necklace/Of his bones we shall make flutes/Of his skin we shall make a drum/Later, we'll dance."[89]

Zoomorphic Motifs. Zoomorphic motifs symbolize a cult to creatures found in the three main geographical areas of Peru. The most frequently portrayed are fishes, seabirds, frogs and foxes from the coast; condors, felines and camelids from the highlands; and caymans, serpents and monkeys from the tropical Amazonian lowlands to the east of the Andes.

The inspiration for these themes seems to have been fourfold: from legends and myths, which frequently deal with colorful creatures (Amaru, the huge two-headed snake in *Huarochiri,* for example); from the pronounced feline cult of Chavin and Tiahuanaco; from the totemic, talismanic and instinctive primeval power that ancient peoples have traditionally assigned to zoomorphic beings; and from the homage and veneration accorded to the animal world in ancient Peru.

The reasons for such veneration were varied, the chronicler Garcilaso de la Vega tells us. The coastal people worshipped the whale because of its size, as well as whatever fish provided them with the most bountiful sustenance; it might be the minuscule sardine or what was a spotted diamond-shaped fish rather like the sole. The owl was eulogized for the beauty of its eyes and head; the condor because some people considered it the origin of man; foxes and monkeys for their astuteness.[90] A golden fox, the chronicler Calancha narrates, was a guardian of the shrine of Pachacamac. Monkeys assisted in amorous liaisons by providing the gods with aphrodisiacal seeds, and shared with lizards the role of helpers to gods.

Birds were of special significance because of their indispensable role in uniting man, the earth and fishes in a cyclical system of growth and renewal. Seabirds like the cormorant, known in Quechua as *guanay,* ate the protein-rich fish that proliferate off the Peruvian coast because of the cold waters of the Humboldt current.[91] They left their droppings, guano, to accumulate on the offshore islands as piles of a white, chalk-like substance. The chronicler Cieza de León describes how the coastal peoples collected guano to use as fertilizer for the sporadic river-valley areas of the desert coast, and reports that it was considered so valuable by the Incas that they imposed strict regulations regarding use, and severe punishments for violations thereof.[92]

Zoomorphic motifs are often rendered in a serial-imagery pattern. Mantles are decorated with embroidered or woven birds, for example, that are identical in size and shape but whose colors may vary according to rhythmically repeated patterns established by the artist. Often Quechua poems stress a specific leitmotiv with the same insistence as does the weaver, suggesting that textile iconography serves as a graphic metaphor for spoken ideas and thoughts. In the opening forty lines of the first *arawi,* or stanza, of the famed verse drama *Ollantay,* a bird (Tuyallay) is warned insistently in each of 20 alternating lines not to eat a specific type of grain likely to cause its death. The four opening lines indicate the pattern that is followed: "Ama, ppisqua, mikuychu/Tuyallay, Tuyallay,/Nustallapa chajranta/Tuyallay, Tuyallay."[93] Illus. 22, depicting 16 birds, is a type of visual metaphor for this sort of poem.

Serial imagery, whether in zoomorphic or human motifs, likewise emphasizes the prominence of cult objects or personalities. The contemporary United States painter Andy Warhol has used serial imagery in his repeated portrayals of Elvis Presley, Marilyn Monroe, Elizabeth Taylor, Liza Minnelli and others. But whereas these are clearly "Pop" symbols of wealth, sex and power, "high profile" personalities in an overtly secular and materialistic society, the figures in ancient Peruvian textiles represented a totally different type of adulation: one founded on an authentic and profound gratitude to, and respect for, cosmic and divine forces. It is almost as though the state secular and religious authorities deliberately encouraged the repeated portrayal of deities as cult figures, using the textile as a vehicle of propaganda and publicity rather like radio, television or the billboard.

The feline, a ubiquitous presence in Peruvian textiles, is represented as a symbol of grace, speed and power whose voracious jaws, legends say, can devour the moon. The feline has always been surrounded by a magical, mystical aura: the French Symbolist poet Charles Baudelaire wrote of cats, and so did the Irishman William Butler Yeats: "When have I last looked on/the round green eyes and the long wavering bodies/of the dark leopards of the Moon?"[94]

Mythical and Fantastic Motifs. Mythical beings are of three types. Anthropomorphic motifs assume zoomorphic attributes, for example, so that a truncated human figure may have bat claws. Secondly, "composite" figures are those whose combination of human, animal, bird, serpentiform or other characteristics endows them with a fantastic appearance. Finally, there is the dragon motif, which appears in many guises.

How can we account for the first two categories? Aniela Jaffe, a former collaborator with the famed psychologist Carl Jung, has written that when a primitive chief dons an animal mask, or dresses as an animal, he *is* thereby the totem animal. He consequently assumes its intuitive power and demonic strength, with human expression being suppressed. She notes that "in the religion of practically every race, animal attributes are ascribed to the supreme gods: Ganesha, Hindu god of good fortune, has a human body but the head of an elephant. Even the Greek Zeus approaches a girl whom he desires in the form of a swan or an eagle."[95]

These sorts of metamorphoses had practical advantages. The god Cuniraya Viracocha, ardently desiring to fecundate the maiden Cavillaca, whom he found weaving below a tree, changed himself into a bird in order to accomplish his goal.[96] It seems probable, however, that the merging of human and zoomorphic traits in textile art responded above all to the ancient Peruvian world view of Oneness, of an integrated cosmos in which lines of demarcation between the human, divine, animal and inanimate worlds were never clearly drawn. It is also conceivable that there may have been moral overtones implicit in composite mythological beings, such fantastic figures being created to manifest the overwhelming omnipotence of divine power, and as a warning not to provoke the gods. We have no empirical evidence to this effect, but one recalls that in other ancient cultures confrontations with the gods were fraught with untimely consequences. In ancient Greece, when Arachne devised such beautiful weavings that nymphs left their vineyards to come to see them, she was viewed by Minerva (Athena), goddess of weaving, as a rival and was changed by the latter into a spider.

The most dramatic of all fantastic and mythological creatures is the dragon. For Dr. Tello, the dragon ranked

with the sun, moon and their twin children as the creatures of the universe. This dragon, "feeding itself with the blood of sacrificial victims," and sometimes triumphantly carrying trophy heads, evidently had no one specific image.[97] Rather, it appears in many forms: as monstrous creatures inspired by the feline, serpent, lizard and cayman, as winged Pegasus-like images of the type shown in Illus. 13 and as a strangely humped version of a camelid. It may even be related to, or at times synonymous with, the north coast Chimu moon goddess Si, who usually appears in a seated profile position and seems to combine monkey, feline and cayman attributes (Illus. 26).

Natural Phenomena Motifs. There are not many recognizable renditions of the phenomena of nature; we do not know how the ancient Peruvians depicted thunder and lightning, for example, in a graphic sense, unless it was by their often used zigzag linear compositions. The Sun is the cosmic body that emerges as a favorite iconographic theme of several cultures. In Chancay and Chimu painted textiles, it is often a smiling, childlike face, sketched in freehand by the artist with a disarming simplicity. In south soast Huari and Nasca feather textiles it is a majestic presence, usually portrayed in cadmium yellow tones and with the facial characteristics blocked in, often in checkerboard style, in black and white feathers. The background may be either a solid color, one on which crosses or squares appear, or multicolored; red, blue and white are the color generally used in such backgrounds.

In Inca textiles, the sun frequently is reduced to a small symbol, rather than a monumental image. As a geometrically shaped eight- or six-pointed star, it functions as a component element and autonomous design symbol in large compositions (Illus. 14).

Symbolism: Pictographs and Ideograms

Once an object assumes such a simplified or stylized format that its original identity becomes subordinated to its usefulness as a decorative shape, we are dealing with the second category of iconography: symbols composed of pictographs and ideograms. Although the majority of pre-Columbian Peruvian peoples used symbols to some degree in their iconography, it is in the Tiahuanaco, Huari and Inca cultures that this tendency is especially pronounced.

In the case of Tiahuanaco and Huari, the most common pictographs are shown in Diagram 1: (1) a grid of crossed lines, which evolved from the lines originally delineating such objects as hands, feet, wings, etc; (2) a circular shape that becomes elliptical, hexagonal, octagonal or similarly shaped, and that may be either monochrome or bisected into two horizontal or vertical segments (a vertical appendage extending downward from such a shape suggests that its origin was the eye from which tears well in the Gateway central deity figure; the origin of this circular shape may also be the sun); (3) a rectangle, quite clearly the original mouth of a figure, enclosing feline fangs suggested by inverted fangs forming a Z-type letter;[98] (4) a step shape, which is often joined to a curved volute that may be the curvilinear

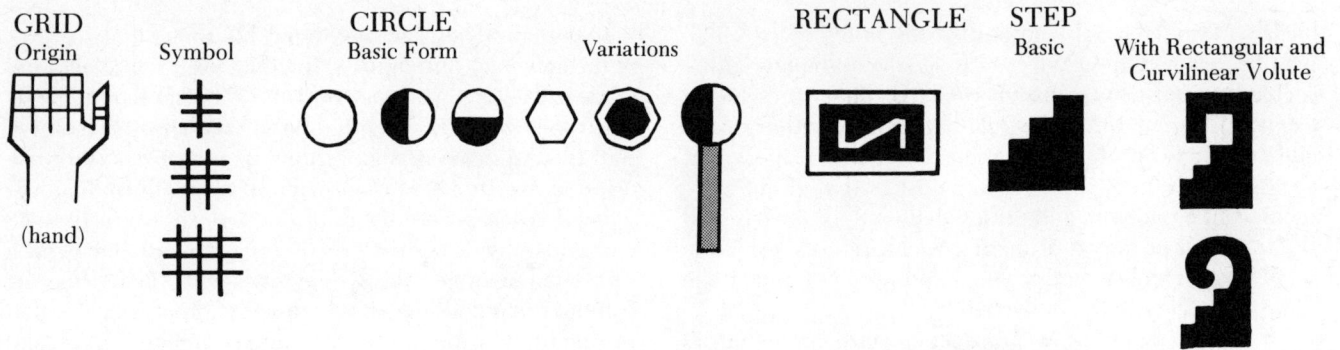

| GRID | | CIRCLE | | RECTANGLE | STEP | |
| Origin | Symbol | Basic Form | Variations | | Basic | With Rectangular and Curvilinear Volute |

(hand)

Diagram 1: Basic Symbols Used in Tiahuanaco and Huari Textile Design.

tail of the feline or, in the Bolivianist Posnansky's view, the merging of earth and sky.[99]

These symbols clearly evolved stylistically, and probably chronologically. Documented evidence is lacking to confirm this but, since these symbols were originally component parts of recognizable figurative motifs, simplification probably occurred with the passage of time. The modular figure became fragmented and the component elements, divested of their original meaning and anatomical relevance, ended up as decorative shapes which the weaver could use to conform with aesthetic dictates of design. All this makes Tiahuanaco and Huari textiles the most cerebral and rhythmically structured of all those of ancient Peru.

With the Incas, who appear to have derived many architectural concepts from their fellow highland Tiahuanaco and Huari peoples, the symbol no longer merely implies association with a recognizable image. It now becomes an ideogram, that is to say a pictographic design clearly representing words or ideas. The most advanced use of ideograms in the pre-Columbian world ocurred in Mexico with the Mayas, some 800 of whose hieroglyphic pictographs have been identified by scholars; in the sixteenth century, the Spanish bishop Diego de Landa succeeded in deciphering the calendrical relevance of many of these pictographs, but not the alphabetical.

The Peruvian Victoria de la Jara concluded in 1967 that "Inca writing is a logographic system using symbols to represent entire words that can be understood without considering the pronunciation." She and the cryptologist Thomas Barthel have reportedly deciphered some 40 of the 400 ideograms which they believe they have identified in Peruvian textiles.[100] However, a more comprehensive analytical contribution has been the relatively recent work of William Burns Glynn, author of the *Calculating Table of the Incas* and the *Key to Deciphering the Secret Writing of the Incas.*[101]

Details of Glynn's methodology are complex and far beyond the scope of this brief text, but the outlines can be briefly synthesized. His basic theory combines phonetic and pictographic aspects, and posits a relationship between the sounds of the numbers 1 to 10 in Quechua and a Quechua alphabet which Glynn presupposes contains ten consonants only; vowels, he suggests, must be interpolated. These ten consonants are generally derived from the letter most emphasized in the pronunciation of any Quechua word. An example will clarify this.

"Seven" in Quechua is *qanchis*, and the stress falls on the *qa*, which provides a *qa, ka, ca* or *k* sound. From analyses of the type indicated below, this particular sound is found to correspond to a shape that is either a square or, when rotated, a diamond. Glynn derives the sound corresponding to these shapes in the following manner.

Using drawings made by the Spanish chronicler Felipe Guaman Poma de Ayala, the only man to leave a detailed graphic account of the period, Glynn focuses on those drawings of Inca rulers whose name Guaman includes on the drawing. For example, a drawing entitled "Manco Capac" (the founder Inca) shows a figure wearing a tunic with three horizontal bands. These repeat continually four series of *tocapus*—squares with ideograms—which Glynn matches up with the four syllable sounds of Manco Capac, as shown in Diagram 2.

Therefore the diagram shows how the diamond (rotated square) shape corresponds to the *qa, ka, ca* or *k* sound. This system may be able to tell us something about Inca textile iconography. Take the characteristic *tocapu* symbol illustrated in Diagram 3A. Many Inca shirts exist of which the upper half is covered with squares enclosing this design, and the lower half consists of striped lines; one is shown in Illus. 56. The way in which Glynn arrives at the interpretation of this *tocapu* design as reading *kapak*, a Quechua word signifying lord, august sovereign or, in Garcilaso de la Vega's words, a person rich in noble virtues, is illustrated in Diagram 3B. The two squares have been completed by

Diagram 2: Illustration from *Boletín de Lima,* 1981, accompanying William Burns Glynn article.

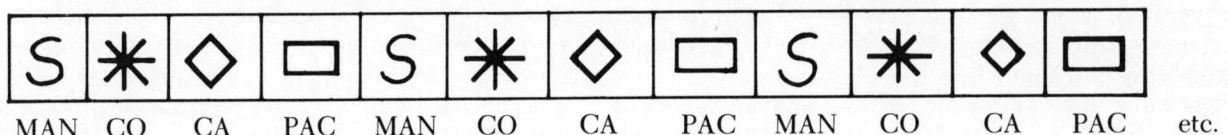

| MAN | CO | CA | PAC | MAN | CO | CA | PAC | MAN | CO | CA | PAC | etc. |

dotted lines, thereby furnishing two *k* sounds. Since the parallel lines were shown by analysis of other iconography to signify a *p*, it merely remains to interpolate a usable vowel—in this case, *a*—between the top *k* and the *p*, and between the *p* and the bottom *k*.

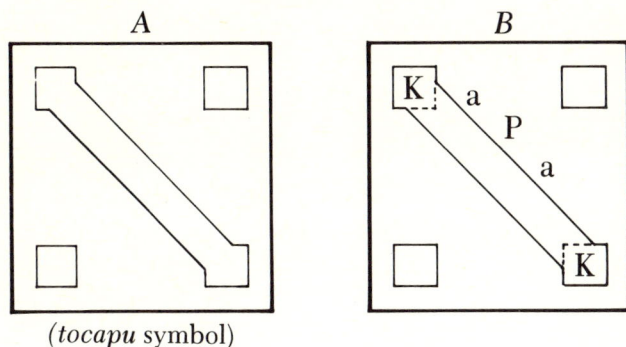

(tocapu symbol)

Diagram 3: Illustration from *Boletín de Lima*, 1981, accompanying William Burns Glynn article.

So, what we have here is a shirt telling us repeatedly that the wearer is being exalted as *kapak:* a noble by rank and a person of virtuous character.

How valid is Glynn's hypothesis? Poma de Ayala published his chronicle between 1587 and 1615, well after the Spanish Conquest; so one has to hope that the information that he originally collected about the Inca rulers—on which Glynn bases his work—was correct initially and not affected by the passage of time. Glynn's methodology leaves certain questions unanswered, but constitutes an original challenge to a difficult and controversial subject.

Apart from their communicative significance, Inca textiles are visually very imposing. The Incas constructed many of their textiles with the same hierarchic order, the same pragmatic equilibrium and the same attention to detail with which they organized their state. There is not much figurative iconography in Inca weaving, but instead there are the *tocapu* compositions, some of which are an exhilarating pot-pourri of every imaginable sign, symbol and ideogram miraculously forged together into a harmonious allover design.

Nonfigurative and Abstract Compositions

For the purposes of this discussion, nonfigurative compositions refer to those in which geometric shapes derived from realistic origins function as autonomous elements of design. A group of those shapes most conspicuously employed in nonfigurative textile compositions is illustrated in Diagram 4.

Abstract compositions, on the other hand, refer to surfaces covered with pure color: a mantle of one color field, for example, or a sleeveless shirt with two primary colors juxtaposed.

Nonfigurative and abstract textiles appear at first glance to have evolved chronologically from pictographs and ideograms, and as a logical consequence of the process of abbreviation, simplification and geometric stylization carried out over many centuries. Empirical evidence, however, does not adequately support this hypothesis of a chronological stylistic development, since nonfigurative textile designs occur as early as the Paracas period.

Nonfigurative imagery is characterized by the same design conventions that were found in figurative and symbolic iconography: allover designs, serial imagery, the single monumental image, combinations of differently shaped images, and so on. For the artists of ancient Peru, each of the geometric shapes illustrated in Diagram 4 offered endless compositional possibilities, which they celebrated with an indefatigable spirit of imagination and innovation. The range of their creativity can be appreciated by examining how merely one shape—the rectangle—was graphically treated in a group of south coast Nasca textiles.

In its most basic textile format, the rectangle comprises a mantle, sleeveless shirt or other item of a single color of uniform gradation. When two rectangles of differing colors are juxtaposed to form such a garment—in the case of Illus. 61 it is a sleeveless shirt—the twin-rectangle banner motif (so called because of its resemblance to flags and pennants of medieval heraldry) is formed. This twin-rectangle nucleus serves as the basis for numerous modifications and adaptations, as shown in Illus. 62 and 63. The composition in which the twin rectangle is surrounded by a periphery of checkerboard squares, usually of three differing colors, is an especially dramatic one visually.

A group of rectangles of similar size and shape may also be used to form an impressive surface design, as in Illus. 60. Here color serves to create a lyrical and harmonious overall composition.

The rectangle, when elongated beyond a certain point, assumes a new configurative identity: that of the bar, band or "barry" (broad stripe). In Diagram 5A, which corresponds to Illus. 65, the broad bands are still clearly extended rectangles. The Nasca shawl in Diagram 5B, however, is bisected vertically and in an off-center area by what is clearly a narrow stripe. In Illus. 66, the repeated pencil-thin stripes of vivid colors comprise a linear pattern evocative of a Moroccan *souk*, a boldly painted Riviera awning from a Matisse picture or a large striped canvas of the twentieth-century United States artist Gene Davis.

Detailed examination of the way in which other geometric shapes were used in multiple manners provides further clues to the restlessly creative spirit of the Andean weaver. The step motif, for example, is illustrated in some of its many variations in Illus. 67–71. Certain cultures favored specific shapes; the Incas, for example, showed special predilection for the diamond, and for a bold V-motif, which they generally employed below the neck area on shirts.

The range of mood in nonfigurative imagery is from the vigorous and robust to the fragile and delicate, from the simple to the complex, from the static to the dynamic. Stark monolithic images loom with monumental grandeur: solid and permanent, as austere as a Minimal painting and as solemn as a Bach fugue. In serial-imagery compositions, shapes achieve a hierarchic presence in which order prevails

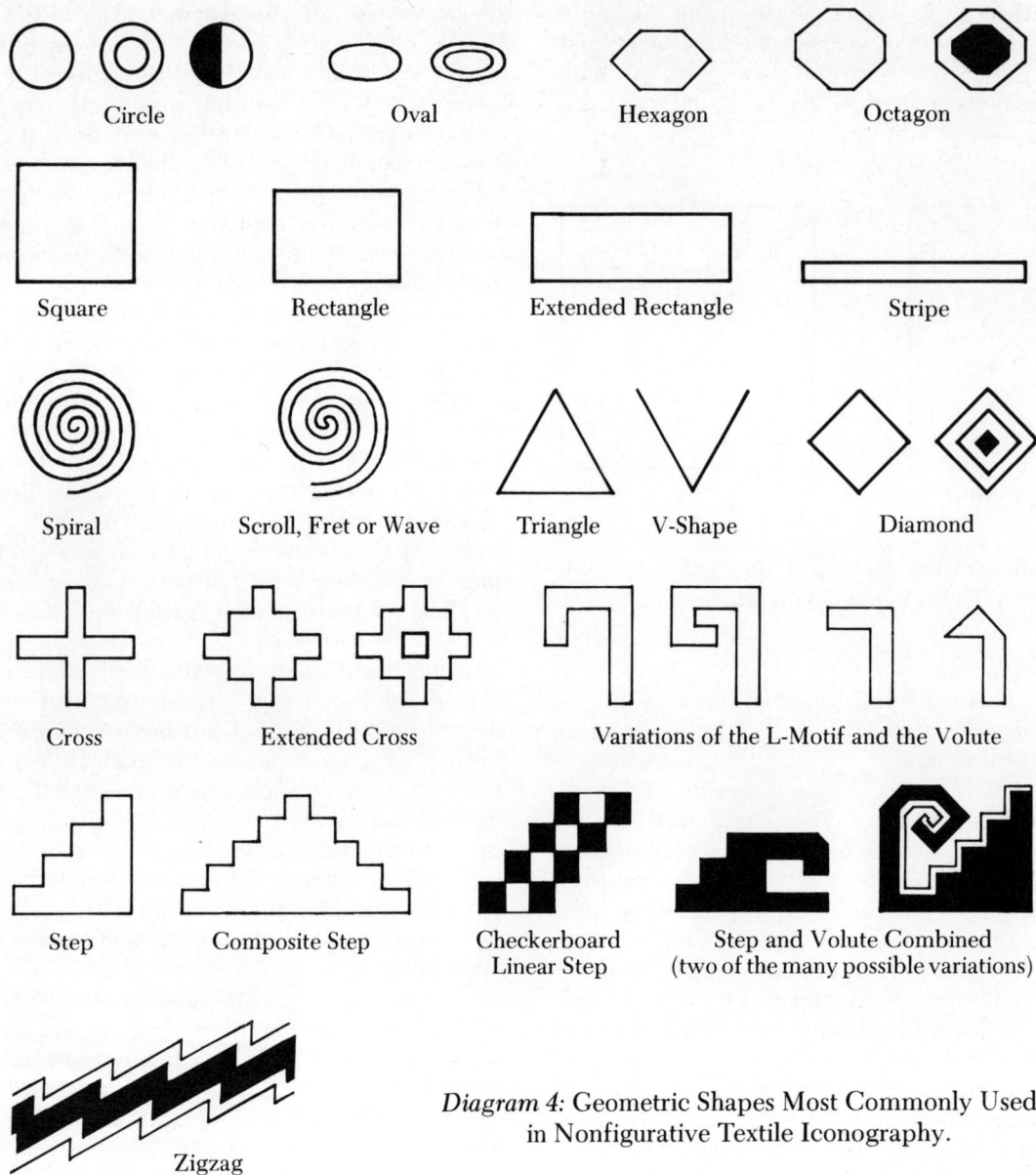

Circle   Oval   Hexagon   Octagon

Square   Rectangle   Extended Rectangle   Stripe

Spiral   Scroll, Fret or Wave   Triangle   V-Shape   Diamond

Cross   Extended Cross   Variations of the L-Motif and the Volute

Step   Composite Step   Checkerboard Linear Step   Step and Volute Combined (two of the many possible variations)

Zigzag

Diagram 4: Geometric Shapes Most Commonly Used in Nonfigurative Textile Iconography.

and logic is affirmed. In tie-dye pieces of vivid colors, the decorative surface pulsates as myriad circles dart frenetically through space and cavort in a crescendo of explosive energy. More meditative works invite contemplation. Certain feather textiles convey a sense of the silent and the sublime with such transcendental grandeur that they evoke a religious presence and recall the painter Piet Mondrian's words: "The abstract is inwardness brought to its clearest definition, or externality interiorized to the highest degree."[102]

Perhaps this is one of the guiding factors that prompted the artists of ancient Peru so frequently to eschew the realistic, the illustrative and the anecdotal and to seek through abstraction a way to express absolutely their sense of the cosmic and the divine. "Realistic representations would not have attained the greatness synonymous with the

divine," one scholar has written of Tiahuanaco textiles.[103] Actually, most nonfigurative and abstract art is almost always related to nature, to the human and to the animal world. So much so, says Aniela Jaffe, that abstract paintings often turn out to be more or less exact images of nature itself.[104] For the twentieth-century Swiss painter Paul Klee, whose work is so often evocative of Peruvian textiles, this dialogue with nature was indispensable for his work.[105]

The omnipresent manifestations of nature, combined with human intervention, must inevitably have influenced the artists of ancient Peru: the *andén* (Sp), for example, the irrigation terrace along Andean slopes, looks in profile like the step design, and the *ayllu* plot of communal land in the Inca period normally had a square or rectangular configuration. Such physical structures appear related to nonfigurative textile iconography. "All the planes appear to

20

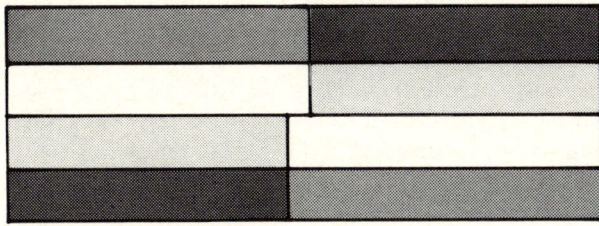

A

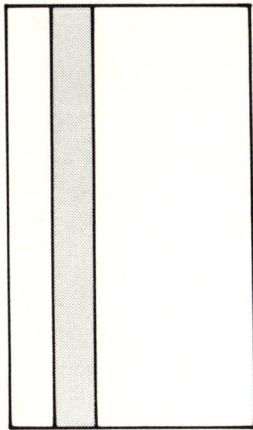

B

Diagram 5: The Rectangle Becomes a Stripe.

represent constructions, spaces enclosed by walls, urbanization plans, areas of land, that is to say an association with irrigation and the parcelling of land."[106]

Such other man-made objects as mats, baskets and the like, fashioned from totora reed and similar materials, may also have stimulated abstract designs. Thus geometrical shapes may "owe their origin to the technique of basketry, to the interlacing of twigs, grasses, roots, vegetable fibers, etc. Scrolls, meanders, frets and other geometrical figures are common to the decorative art of many peoples."[107]

Weaving itself, which stresses vertical, horizontal and diagonal linear structures, undoubtedly contributed to the stylizing of forms into geometric shapes; so too, probably, did the routine experience of working with similar motifs during hundreds of years. As for the influence of looms, Alan Sawyer's penetrating analysis of the way in which the highland Huari loom inevitably imposed design constraints by causing "lateral compression" at the borders of the textile has been instrumental in explaining why many Huari motifs have become fragmented and distorted.

Finally the infallible eye, the unerring sense of design and the precocious sophistication of composition may have combined to produce an art that corresponded to a criterion of beauty very close in certain ways to that of our century.

The Aesthetics of Ancient Peruvian Textile Art

The extent to which twentieth-century art has been influenced by, or shares affinities with, African, Oceanic, European folk and even Indonesian art has been extensively documented. This is not the case with Peruvian textile art, which is perhaps the closest of all in feeling and expression to our century.

The reasons are clear. First, exhibitions of Peruvian textiles have been comparatively rare, and those held in museums tend to emphasize archeological and technical, rather than artistic, aspects. Secondly, only in the last two decades have major publications appeared in Europe, Japan and South America with extensive color reproductions revealing the scope of Peruvian textiles as works of art. Thirdly, as long as conventional "easel painting" was considered the criterion of true art, one could expect a certain reluctance to recognize textiles as art. It is only the radical changes since World War II regarding norms of artistic expression that have effectively negated such views. And finally, since much of the art with which textiles share notable design affinities is itself relatively recent, there has been little time or opportunity to establish comparisons.

These affinities are evident in the three categories of textile iconography. Figurative textile themes are closest to three major manifestations of twentieth-century art: Expressionism, Fantasy and Surrealism, and Pop art. Ideography and pictographic art resemble constructivist movements. And nonfigurative textile iconography approximates various color-field, stripe, geometric, hard-edge, minimal and soft-edge post-World War II schools of artistic expression.

The suggestion of drama and emotion implicit in Expressionism is especially discernible in Peruvian textile art, in view of its earlier mentioned tendency to depict figurative motifs essentially as objective graphic symbols. Thus, in the case of the looming monumental figures with leering visage and grotesque mien, it is as though the ancient weaver had been transported by time machine into the *angst* and subconscious torment so viscerally portrayed by a host of twentieth-century painters: the Norwegian Edvard Munch, the German Emil Nolde and the Belgian James Ensor, all of whom make use of often frightening mask themes; Karel Appel and Asger Jorn, of the COBRA group;[108] the Frenchman Jean Dubuffet, whose monstrous figures with contorted stances, disproportionate limbs and gaping expressions echo atavistically the art of children and the mentally ill; and, most recently, Jean Michel Basquiat, whose graffiti-like Expressionism has imposed its presence on the New York art world of the 1980s.

Some Peruvian textile art evokes the same sort of simplicity. Children, said the painter Kandinsky, are essentially creatures who build directly from the secret of their perceptions, and from the intuitive expression of the interior essence of things.[109] As for the art of the mentally ill, its characteristics are the extension of the human features, especially the eyes and mouth, "into ornamental linear motifs which are then, in neglect of their original intentions, elaborated for their own decorative values."[110]

Although differences in comparative size of motifs are noted—the standing figures in Illus. 24, for example, are notably taller than the llamas at their sides—there is no attempt to use perspective to depict a figure in the foreground as significantly larger than one in the background. In fact, since backgrounds as we know them are not used, we must assume that differences in the size of figures on the same plane either reflect hierarchic importance or are dictated by compositional needs.

Traditional values of anatomical realism are also rejected, and one gets what Goldwater calls "intellectual realism": the arbitrarily selective exaggeration by the artist of those aspects of the body—the head, for example—which are considered to be especially important.[111] This deliberate distortion is a recurring characteristic in Peruvian textile iconography.

This directness, with its emphasis upon the fundamental, often imbues ancient Peruvian figurative images with a sense of primeval forces incarnate. If such images are close graphically to European Expressionism, it is in the work of two twentieth-century painters of the Americas, the Cuban Wifredo Lam and the Mexican Rufino Tamayo, that they find a kindred philosophic spirit. Is this coincidence attributable to their backgrounds, to their sharing of a common American heritage? Many of Tamayo's motifs are drawn from pre-Columbian Mexico, and some of them reflect ancient Andean beliefs. His painting *Dogs Barking at the Moon* portrays a theme reminiscent of the Peruvian legend that the barking of dogs kept the moon from falling from the heavens. With Lam, the primeval and mystical surge out of hallucinatory images of strange masks and idols.

In the realm of fantasy, the works of Paul Klee, Joan Miró, William Baziotes and Marc Chagall remind us most of Peruvian textile iconography. All share a proclivity for the fanciful and whimsical idea, and for the unconventional composition; and so we find figures flying through the clouds on enchanted journeys in Chagall paintings, or amoeba-like squiggles in a Miró canvas. This may seem surrealistic to us, but when that sort of theme was used by an ancient Peruvian weaver it almost certainly corresponded to his untrammeled and untainted world-view. What was possible for him, alas, is no longer possible for our twentieth-century mind saturated with technical, scientific and rational logic.

Symbols and ideograms in modern art have occurred in both structured and unstructured formats. Constructivism is evident in the work of the twentieth-century United States artist Alfred Jensen and in that of the Uruguayan Joaquín Torres García, who reduces clocks, ships, fishes, etc. to simplified shapes, then locates them within informal squares or rectangles in a composition that is mentally arbitrary, but graphically ordered. The early pictographic art of the United States artist Adolph Gottlieb, certain works of Klee, the elliptical dots of Larry Poons—all these suggest at times designs found in Tiahuanaco, Huari or Inca textiles.

Unstructured symbols are found not only in contemporary Western art, but also in African textiles, especially those of the Bakuba. One finds symbols and ideograms scurrying breathlessly across the textile surface or floating in imaginary space. Huari tie-dye textiles, as well as painted pieces from Paracas, Nasca, Chimu and Chancay, often create the same sort of mood.

Finally, in nonfigurative compositions, the most dramatic examples of contemporary art with clear affinities to textile designs of ancient Peru occur in the United States in the painting after World War II. These are the stripe paintings of Kenneth Noland, Morris Louis, Gene Davis and Barnett Newman; the squares within squares of Josef Albers, or the diamonds within diamonds, or V's within V's, of Noland and Frank Stella shaped canvases; the color-field compositions of Ellsworth Kelly; and the spare designs of certain Minimal painters.

Thus in ancient Peru and in the twentieth century artists have often arrived at graphic designs and compositions with marked aesthetic similarities; but whereas the pre-Columbian weaver proceeded from an intuitive sense and an autochthonous environment, the modern painter has emerged from a formalized intellectual tradition where cerebral interchanges between continents, schools and movements have constantly injected new creative stimuli. So, although the finished work of the Andean and modern artist frequently seems alike, the means, method and mentality used in the creative process are totally different.

They are different, above all, because their environments are so totally disparate. The French painter Henri Matisse once remarked: "We are born with the sensibility of a given epoch of civilization. We are not masters of what is produced; it is imposed upon us."[112] And the sensibility of twentieth-century Paris, London and New York, where modern art largely developed surrounded by urban technology, is totally alien to the rural world of the ancient Andes. "Behind the terrifying, crazy tempo of technical evolution," wrote the eminent theologian Emil Brunner in 1946, "there is all the insatiability of secularized man . . . not believing in God or eternal life."[113] There have undoubtedly been occasional major modern artists who are deeply religious: one thinks of Rouault and Manessier. But the representative mood of contemporary artistic expression is best summarized in Kandinsky's early twentieth-century comment in *On the Spiritual in Art* that "Heaven is empty, God is dead," or the Italian de Chirico's reference to a "metaphysical void." It is this sort of attitude that finally caused "the cleavage between Christianity and modern art."[114]

This is why a painter like Jean Dubuffet, whose figurative themes often evoke Peruvian textile motifs, is inspired by a different philosophic process. His work, the noted Mexican author Octavio Paz has commented, is "not a celebration of reality but a confrontation with it, an art of vengeance, not of love. It is not a ritual but the macabre interplay of irony and despair."[115]

The ancient Peruvian textile artist, on the other hand, celebrated the reality of his cosmos, demonstrated his devotion to his deities through his art and confronted an often unfathomable world with an optimism and faith reflected in an assiduous attention to ritual and religious ceremony.

Sixty years have passed since Julio C. Tello, accompanied by his United States colleague Samuel K. Lothrop, discovered the great Necropolis cemetery of Paracas.[116] The burial site of Cerro Colorado, today a stark, unprepossessingly austere hilly outcrop of spare rocks and scarred sand, seems strangely irrelevant: small scattered rectangular peripheries of obliquely shaped stones dispersed almost disparagingly over some 260 square meters. "Nothing besides remains," wrote the English poet Shelley; "Round the decay/Of that colossal wreck, boundless and bare,/The loose and level sands stretch far away." But his words evoke not so much Ozymandias as they do Cerro Colorado. The humility of its tombs is disturbing, the silence broken only by the impatient wind's somber reminder of human frailty and transient splendor. The vanished nobility who once wore those spectacular textiles are as old as the words on a pre-Christian Roman sacrificial font: "Sol redit, tempus numquam." The sun returns, but time never.[117]

In the early morning, the roseate hues of northeasterly dawn bathe the gentle slopes of Cerro Colorado with soft golden light. But as noon approaches, in the burnished heat of summer, the light becomes incandescent, reflecting eerily off the surrounding dunes. Beyond the foot of the hill, the resonant cobalt blue of the bay of Paracas quivers, juxtaposed against the intense chrome yellow of the sands and the ultramarine red of the cliffs. Refractions of pink signal the presence of flamingos, whose feathers once graced resplendent textiles. Overhead, an occasional condor soars down from Andean peaks in search of prey.

The majesty of the environment evokes the matchless splendor of bygone days, of incomparable mantles peopled by immanent deities and mortals in harmony with their cosmos. To experience these textiles we need to go back in time, to understand how Andean man lived and thought. How different a world view was his from the somber vision of twentieth-century man, from the scepticism expressed in the opening lines of Rainer Maria Rilke's *Duino Elegies*: "If I should cry out/Who would hear me up there/Amid the Angelic orders?"[118]

The weaving artists of ancient Peru, deeply aware of their reciprocal relationships with nature and the gods, counted on the Upper World and Lower Interior World to heed their call. They believed that divine response to their invocations was contingent upon a display of respect and veneration by mortals: hence the iconography of their textiles. It is for this reason that such textiles, glowing with luminescent colors and vibrant designs, radiate a profound, ineffable faith and a transcendental sense of cosmic splendor.

NOTES

Works listed in the Bibliography on page 26 are cited here in abbreviated form only.

1. "Cosa de espanto ver su hechura, sin parecer hilo alguno," wrote Pedro Pizarro (see Bibliography). Francisco de Xeres (see Bibliography), p. 31.

2. Pablo Neruda, *Alturas de Machu Picchu*, 1972, second ed. 1977, Editorial Losada, Buenos Aires. Neruda's lines referring to textiles are: "Aquí la hebra dorada salio de la vicuña / a vestir los amores, los túmulos, las madres, / el rey, las oraciones, los guerreros" (p. 26) and "hasta la tela de materia radiante" (p. 47).

3. Guano, from the Quechua word *guanay*, meaning cormorant, refers to the droppings of sea birds which were used as fertilizer. Quechua, the language spoken by the Incas and still used today by millions of highland Andean Indians, was originally known as Runa Simi but was given the name Quechua by the Spanish priest Fray Domingo de Santo Tomás.

4. Paul Marcoy (see Bibliography), Half-Volume I, p. 4.

5. Robert Goldwater, *Primitivism in Modern Art*, 1938. Reprint: Knopf and Random House, New York, 1967, p. 7.

6. M. D. C. Crawford, "Peruvian Fabrics" (see Bibliography), Chapters III and IV, pp. 53–193.

7. Leroy H. Appleton, *American Indian Design and Decoration*, Dover Publications, New York, 1971, p. 4 (reprint of *Indian Art of the Americas*, 1950).

8. Dr. J. Maes, *La Psychologie de l'Art Nègre*, Ipek II, 1926, pp. 275, 283: "Efforçons-nous au contraire de comprendre la psychologie de l'art nègre et nous finirons par en pénétrer toute la beauté et toute la vie!"

9. The most prominent Spanish chroniclers are represented in the Bibliography. They often differ regarding the spelling of proper names; Pachacutec, for example, is also spelled Pachacuti.

10. Valcarcel deals with this theme in the first part of his essay listed in the Bibliography.

11. Valcarcel, pp. 78–85.

12. Louis Baudin (see Bibliography), p. 24.

13. Rebeca Carrión Cachot de Girard (see Bibliography), p. 9.

14. The best discussions of *mallqui* (also spelled *malqui*) are found in Valcarcel, pp. 30 and 83–87, and María Rostworowski de Diez Canseco, pp. 61–71 (see Bibliography).

15. See Rostworowski, pp. 21–71, for an excellent distinction between major and minor deities.

16. Jesús Lara (see Bibliography), p. 159.

17. Rostworowski (see Bibliography) cites the Spanish priest Francisco de Avila (see note 21) as the source of this information, p. 37.

18. Miguel Caballo de Valboa (see Bibliography).

19. This legend is cited by Juan Cristóbal Calvete de Estrella (see Bibliography).

20. The chronicler Pablo José de Arriaga (see Bibliography) mentions that "when they went from the village of Huaco to obtain guano from the islands off Huaura, they first made an offering, pouring chicha onto the beach so that their boats would have a safe trip, and also fasting for two days; and when they arrived at the islands, they paid homage to the huaca (holy place) of Huamancantac, who was the Lord of Guano, and after returning to port they again fasted for two days and then sang, danced and drank" (cited in Valcarcel, p. 148). Elizabeth P. Benson, *The Mochica*, Thames and Hudson, London, 1972, provides useful information on such Mochica deities as Aiapaec.

21. See pp. 68, 80 of the Arguedas translation of *Dioses y Hombres de Huarochiri* (in Bibliography, under Anonymous).

22. Kenneth Clark, *Civilisation*, Harper and Row, New York, 1969, pp. 8–80.

23. Ernst Vatter, *Religiöse Plastik der Naturvölker*, Frankfurter-Verlag, Frankfurt-am-Main, 1926, p. 5.

24. Alan Lapiner (see Bibliography), p. 22.

25. Garcilaso de la Vega, Inca, *The Incas* (see Bibliography), p. 138.

26. Alfredo Taullard (see Bibliography), p. 52.

27. *Huarochiri* (see note 21), p. 25: "Y muchos más los maestros tejedores que tenían una labor tan difícil . . . ."

28. Xeres (see Bibliography), p. 28, on the Cajamarca buildings. On the farming-out system of raw materials, Juan Polo de Ondegardo (see Bibliography) writes on p. 66 of "the wool which was distributed by the community to each person who needed it for his clothing and for that of his women and children," and on p. 127 of the fact that "no Indian had to contribute the materials for making his own clothing."

29. Bernabé Cobo (see Bibliography) classifies the range of textiles in Book XIV, Chap. XI, pp. 258–59, and comments: "De esta ropa se vestían los reyes, los grandes señores y toda la nobleza del reino, y no la podía usar el común del pueblo."

30. Juan de Betanzos (see Bibliography), Chap. XIII.

31. Ann P. Rowe, *Costumes and Featherwork* . . . (see Bibliography), p. 18.

32. The best descriptions of annealing and repoussé in pre-Columbian art appear in André Emmerich, *Sweat of the Sun and Tears of the Moon*, University of Washington Press, Seattle, 1965, pp. 6, 30, 37, 158–59, and in Lapiner (see Bibliography), p. 262.

33. John O'Neill (see Bibliography), pp. 145–85.

34. Victor W. Von Hagen (see Bibliography), p. 81, on the Amanteca. For the information on feathers, see Felipe Guaman Poma de Ayala (see Bibliography), p. 207.

35. Charles Gallenkamp, *Maya*, David McKay Co., New York, 1959, p. 180.

36. *The World of the American Indian*, National Geographic Society, Washington, D.C., 1974.

37. Xeres, p. 53, on Atahuallpa. The lines in Rubén Darío's poem are: "Ellos eran soberbios, leales y francos, / ceñidas las cabezas de raras plumas."

38. Various chroniclers write of the magic and witchcraft associated with feathers and textiles. Cobo recounts the habit of caressing the Inca ruler's face with the feathers of the *tocto* bird; de Valboa describes the *runatingui* and Pablo José de Arriaga describes the methods used by *mosocs*.

39. Bartolomé de las Casas, *Apologética Historia Sumaria*, ca. 1550. Reprint: Biblioteca de Autores Españoles (BAE), No. 13, Editorial M. Menéndez Pelayo, Madrid, 1909.

40. Bishop Alonso de la Peña Montenegro, *Itinerario para Parrochos de Indios* . . ., J. F. De Buendía, Madrid, 1668.

41. Alan Sawyer, *Tiahuanaco Tapestry Design* (see Bibliography).

42. Eduard Versteylen, "Archeological Textiles in Peru and the Importance of Establishing a National Textile Museum," pp. 95–101 of *Irene Emery Roundtable on Museum Textiles, 1974 Proceedings, Archeological Textiles*, Textile Museum, Washington, D.C., 1975, p. 96; and Lapiner (see Bibliography), pp. 74, 75 and 96.

43. Ann P. Rowe, *Warp-Patterned Weaves of the Andes* (see Bibliography), p. 11.

44. Jane P. Dwyer, "The Chronology and Iconography of Paracas-Style Textiles," in *Junius B. Bird Pre-Columbian Textile Conference*, Textile Museum, Washington, D.C., 1979, pp. 105–28.

45. The *tullpuni* Andean dyeing process was so described by Padre Huerta, in *Arte de la Lengua Quechua General de los Indios de este Reyno del Perú* (1616). Cited by Rogger Ravines (see Bibliography), p. 262.

46. Mary Elizabeth King, *Ancient Peruvian Textiles* . . . (see Bibliography), p. 1.

47. Rowe, *Costumes and Featherwork* (see Bibliography), pp. 7–34.

48. Rafael Larco Herrera, *Peru*, Archaeologia Mundi, Nagel, Geneva, 1966, p. 191.

49. Baudin (see Bibliography), p. 98.

50. Lapiner comments on the famous Chimu "prisoner" textile, reportedly found on the hacienda Moyope in Peru in 1951 and believed originally to have been about 105 feet long and 6 feet wide (see Bibliography), p. 263.

51. Murra, *La Función del Tejido* (see Bibliography), pp. 145–70.

52. Dwyer, *op. cit*, p. 105.

53. Various chroniclers mention the presence of images on fiesta days being richly clad in feather plumes and textiles. Among them: Cobo (see Bibliography), pp. 156–57, and Betanzos (see Bibliography), Chap. XI, p. 33.

54. Valcarcel (see Bibliography), pp. 136–38 and 150–61, summarizes the different accounts that chroniclers furnish of the *capocha*. The similarly sounding *qhapaq hucha* is described by Betanzos (see Bibliography), Chap. XI, p. 33.

55. Valcarcel, p. 165, mentions Arriaga as his source.

56. See Fray Martín de Murúa, *Historia del Origen y Genealogía de los Reyes Incas del Perú* (copy of Loyola manuscript, 1600–1611). Reprint: Instituto Santo Toribio de Mongrovejo, Madrid, 1946, Vol. II, Chap. LVII, p. 306 for discussion of effigy hanging. Guaman Poma de Ayala mentions the magical aspects of black and white thread.

57. The shamans also carried round stones on which were painted designs of snakes, pumas, frogs, etc., according to Valcarcel, p. 142, who cites Murúa as the source of information for the *cuscoviza*, also called *huallavisa* or *supavisa*.

58. Murra, *La Función del Tejido* (see Bibliography), p. 153.

59. Fernando S. Santisteban, *El Simbolismo del Rojo en los Ritos Funerarios de la Pre-Historia Andina*, Scientia et Praxis, No. 12, Universidad Nacional Mayor de San Marcos, Lima, 1977, p. 67.

60. Charles Wiener (see Bibliography), p. 54.

61. Polo de Ondegardo (see Bibliography) discusses the *warachikuy*, pp. 200, 201.

62. Murúa, *op. cit.*, Chap. XXXIII, p. 240.

63. Murra, *La Función* (see Bibliography), pp. 157–61.

64. Cabello (see Bibliography), Chap. XXVI, pp. 408 and 413, describes the incident, stating that Huascar, "taking the clothes that his brother had sent him . . ., hurled them into the fire."

65. The Quechua lines are: "Ujman ppachata qonáypaj / Uj qolqeyta rikunánpaj / Nogatari manchanánpaj."

66. Murra, *La Función*, p. 167.

67. Cieza de León thought the *quipus* only recorded romances and legends, but the Spanish authorities believed them to be sources of magic and witchcraft. Item 10 of the 1551 Council of Lima ordered them removed, and the 1583 Council ordered them burned.

68. Mark Strand (see Bibliography), p. 11.

69. Baudin, pp. 122–37.

70. Xeres, p. 48. Pedro Pizarro called the Inca emblem of sovereignty the *llautu*, and described it as "made of plaits of colored wool . . . worn in the manner of a crown."

71. Valcarcel, p. 165, cites Arriaga as the source of information on the Parianas, who wore fox skins over their heads. Xeres, p. 53, describes the checkerboard livery.

72. Pedro Pizarro (see Bibliography), p. 195: "No podré decir los depósitos . . . de todos géneros de ropa y vestidos que en este reino se hacían y usaban."

73. Eugenio Yacovleff and J. C. Muelle, "Un Fardo Funerario de Paracas," *Revista del Museo Nacional*, III, Lima, 1934, pp. 63–153.

74. Julio C. Tello, *Paracas* (see Bibliography), p. 48.

75. Baudin, pp. 64–69, points out that each community's terrain was divided between the sun god, the Inca and the community itself, and that such land allocated for use by the people was for usufruct, not ownership.

76. Polo de Ondegardo (see Bibliography), pp. 65, 66: "e visitanlos para ver si lo avian hecho rropa e castigauan al que se descuidaua . . . ."

77. Pedro de Cieza de León, *Tercera Parte* . . . (see Bibliography), Book II, Chap. XVIII, pp. 59–60.

78. Inigo Ortiz de Zúñiga, *Visita de la Provincia León de Huanuco en 1562*, Universidad Nacional H. Valdizan, Huanuco, I, 1967, p. 243; II, 1972, p. 24.

79. Lt. Ruiz, of Moguer, the pilot, discovered the Bay of San Mateo and the Isle of Gallo, and encountered the native raft with cotton and woolen cloths. Ruiz's voyages are discussed in Xeres, pp. 6–12, and Xeres was probably the author of the five-page descriptive manuscript, Codex CXX in the Imperial Library, Vienna, which was reportedly forwarded to King Charles I, then also Holy Roman Emperor as Charles V. The excerpts from the manuscript are translated by John Hemming (see Bibliography), pp. 25, 547.

80. Agustín de Zarate (see Bibliography), Book II, Chap. IX, p. 481. The room destroyed was "una sala llena de muy rica ropa, que alli tenían desde el tiempo de Huayna Capac."

81. Xeres, p. 54: "I know well how you have . . . taken the cloth from my storehouses."

82. Maurice Denis, *Art et Critique,* 23 August 1890. Similar ideas were expressed by Albert Aurier in the *Mercure de France,* March 1891: "The artist must carry out a reasoned stylization . . . in his work use only lines, forms and colors which seem to state clearly the meaning of the object . . . exaggerate, attenuate, distort them . . . according to the needs of the Idea to be expressed."

83. Jane P. Dwyer, *Iconography and Chronology in Paracas and Nasca Textiles,* University of California at Berkeley, Dept. of Anthropology, 1971, pp. 196, 197, 202, 203.

84. Jerrold Morris, *On the Enjoyment of Modern Art,* New York Graphic Society, Greenwich, Conn., 1968, pp. 30, 34, 51.

85. John Coplans, *Serial Imagery,* Pasadena Art Museum, 1968/69, pp. 10-12.

86. Rostworowski (see Bibliography) discusses these concepts in considerable depth.

87. Strand, p. 29.

88. Max Uhle, *Die alten Kulturen* (see Bibliography); and *Los Geroglifos* (see Bibliography), p. 199.

89. Strand, p. 22.

90. Garcilaso de la Vega, *Comentarios Reales de los Incas,* Ediciones Peisa, Lima, Tomo I, p. 36.

91. Von Hagen (see Bibliography), gives a thorough account of Humboldt's activities and discoveries, and of the ecology of the Pacific coast of Peru.

92. Pedro de Cieza de León, *Parte primera* (see Bibliography), pp. 222-23, recounts (author's translation): "Offshore, various islands are plentifully inhabited by sea lions. The local Indians travel there in rafts, and collect large quantities of bird droppings from the top of the rocks. They use these supplies to fertilize the fields which they sow, and find the product so advantageous that normally barren land turns out to be fertile; in fact, failure to use these bird droppings as fertilizer means that little corn will be harvested. These Indians could really not maintain themselves, if it were not for these droppings left by the birds, and so they value the product highly . . . ."

93. Lara (see Bibliography), pp. 167-68.

94. From the poem *Lines Written in Dejection,* in M. L. Rosenthal, *Selected Poems and Two Plays of William Butler Yeats,* Macmillan, New York, 1962, p. 53.

95. Aniela Jaffe, "Symbolism in the Visual Arts," in Carl G. Jung, *Man and His Symbols,* Aldus Books, London, and Doubleday, New York, 1964, p. 237.

96. *Huarochiri,* pp. 26-27.

97. Julio C. Tello, *Wiracocha* (see Bibliography); and *Origen y Desarrollo* (see Bibliography), pp. 26-27.

98. Lapiner, p. 227.

99. Arthur Posnansky (see Bibliography) provides numerous creative interpretations of symbols.

100. Victoria de la Jara, "Vers le Déchiffrement des Ecritures Anciennes du Pérou," *Science Progrès, la Nature,* No. 3387, Paris, 1967, pp. 241-47.

101. William Burns Glynn, *Una Introducción a la Clave de la Escritura de los Incas,* Separata del Boletín de Lima, Nos. 12, 13, 14, 1981, p. 4.

102. Galerie Beyeler, Basle, *Piet Mondrian,* 1964, p. 44.

103. Ferdinand Anton (see Bibliography), esp. pp. 50-60.

104. Jaffe, *op cit.,* p. 264. Given the omnipresent ties between man and nature in the Andean world, a further comment is relevant: "The square, and often the rectangle, is a symbol of earthbound matter, of the body and of reality" (p. 249).

105. *Ibid.,* p. 264.

106. R. Meyer, *El Arte Pre-Colombino Peruano,* Separata del Boletín de Lima, Nos. 6, 7, 8, 1980.

107. C. W. Mead (see Bibliography), pp. 201-02.

108. COBRA stands for Copenhagen, Brussels and Amsterdam, the cities where the main protagonists of this art movement lived and worked.

109. Goldwater, *op cit.,* p. 192.

110. *Ibid.,* p. 195.

111. *Ibid.,* p. 197, 210.

112. Michel Seuphor, *Abstract Painting,* Harry Abrams, New York, undated, p. 16.

113. Emil Brunner, *Christianity and Civilisation,* Gifford Lectures, University of St Andrews, Nisbet and Co., London, 1958, p. 4.

114. Jaffe, *op cit.,* p. 254.

115. Octavio Paz, "An Art of Transformation," Introduction to *Rufino Tamayo: Myth and Magic,* Guggenheim Foundation, New York, 1979, p. 15.

116. The discovery is described by Dr. Arturo Jiménez Borja, in *Paracas,* Banco de Crédito del Perú, L. L. Editores, Lima, 1983, pp. 11-15.

117. The font is in the private collection of Mr. Lee Elman.

118. Rainer Maria Rilke, *The Duino Elegies,* edited and translated by David Young, W. W. Norton and Co., New York, 1978, p. 1.

BIBLIOGRAPHY

Material dealing with the textiles of ancient Peru is found in four types of literature. First, in historical writing, especially that of the Spanish chroniclers, which mentions the religious, social, political, military, economic and psychological importance of textiles in Andean life. Also included in this historical category is the work of the nineteenth-century archeologists, travelers and explorers who contributed to the rediscovery of the artistic heritage of the pre-Conquest period. The second category is general works treating the architecture and art, either of South America as an entity, or more specifically of Peru and Bolivia. The third type of literature is essentially technical, focusing in detail upon the archeological facets of textiles and upon their weaving techniques. The last type of writing, while frequently touching upon some or all of these categories, is concerned fundamentally with textile iconography and design, compositional interpretation and the examination of the aesthetic aspects of Peruvian textiles as major works of creative art.

In the following bibliography, attention has been directed toward selecting, from the extensive body of material available, a representative sampling of works that satisfactorily address these four categories.

Acosta, José de. *Historia Natural y Moral de las Indias,* Seville, 1590. Trans. C. R. Markham, Hakluyt Society, 1 Ser. 60–1, London, 1880.

Amano, Yoshitaro, and Tsunoyama, Yukihiro. *Textiles of the Pre-Incaic Period* (catalogue of the Amano Collection), Shimogyo-ku, Kyoto, 1977.

Anonymous. *Dioses y Hombres de Huarochiri,* Quechua document discovered in the late sixteenth century by the Spanish priest Francisco de Avila, who translated the first six chapters as *Tratado y Relación de los errores, falsos dioses y otras supersticiones y ritos diabólicos en que vivían los indios de Huarochiri, Mama y Chaclla,* 1608; see Avila, below. A new translation of the complete Quechua manuscript, with an introduction by José María Arguedas, was published by Siglo Veintiuno Argentina Editores, Buenos Aires, in 1966 and reprinted in 1975 in Mexico City.

Anton, Ferdinand. *The Art of Ancient Peru,* Thames and Hudson, London, 1972.

———. *Altindianische Textilkunst aus Peru,* List Verlag, Munich/Leipzig, 1984.

Arriaga, Pablo José. *La Extirpación de la Idolatría en el Perú,* 1621. Reprint: Colección H. Urteaga, Tomo 1, Serie 2, Lima, 1920.

Avila, Francisco de. *Tratado y Relación de los errores, falsos dioses y otras supersticiones y ritos diabólicos en que vivían los indios de Huarochiri, Mama y Chaclla,* 1608. Trans. C. R. Markham as *Narration of the Rites and Laws of the Incas,* Hakluyt Society, 1 Ser. 48, London, 1872, pp. 121–47.

Baessler, Arthur. *Ancient Peruvian Art,* Berlin/New York, 1902/03.

Baudin, Louis. *A Socialist Empire: The Incas of Peru,* D. Van Nostrand Co., Princeton, 1961.

Bennett, Wendell C. *Ancient Arts of the Andes,* Museum of Modern Art, New York, 1954.

——— and Bird, Junius B.: *Andean Cultural History,* American Museum of Natural History, New York, 1949.

Betanzos, Juan de. *Suma y Narración de los Incas que los Indios llamaron Capacuna, que fueron Señores de la ciudad del Cuzco y de toda a ello sujeto.* Reprint: Ed. M. J. de la Espada, Biblioteca Hispano-Ultramarina, Vol. V, Madrid, 1880.

Bird, Junius B. *Art and Life in Old Peru; an Exhibition,* Curator, Vol. 2, American Museum of Natural History, New York, 1962, pp. 145–209.

———. *Peruvian Painting by Unknown Artists,* Center for Inter-American Relations, New York, 1973.

———. "Fibers and Spinning in the Andean Area," in *Junius B. Bird Pre-Columbian Textile Conference,* Textile Museum, Washington, D.C., 1979, pp. 13–19.

——— and Bellinger, Louisa. *Paracas Fabrics and Nasca Needlework, 3rd Century* B.C. *to 3rd Century* A.D. (Textile Museum catalogue raisonné), National Publishing Co., Washington, D.C., 1954.

Cabello de Valboa, Miguel. *Miscelánea Antártica,* 1586. Reprint: Instituto de Etnología, Universidad Nacional Mayor de San Marcos, Lima, 1951.

Calancha, Antonio de la. *Corónica Moralizada del orden de San Agustín en el Perú,* Barcelona, 1639. Reprint: *Crónica Moralizada,* Ignacio Prado Pastor, Lima, 1974.

Calvete de Estrella, Juan Cristóbal. *Rebelión de Pizarro en el Perú, y Vida de Don Pedro Gasca,* 1565–67. Reprint: Biblioteca de Autores Españoles (BAE), Vol. CLXVII, Editorial Atlas, Madrid, 1964.

Carrión Cachot de Girard, Rebeca. *La Religión en el Antiguo Perú,* Lima, 1959.

Castelnau, Francis L. (Comte de Laporte). *Expédition dans les Parties Centrales de l'Amérique du Sud, 3e Partie: Antiquités des Incas et autres peuples anciens,* Paris, 1850–59.

Cieza de León, Pedro de. *Parte primera de la chrónica del Perú,* Seville, 1553. Reprint: Fondo Editorial de la Pontificia Universidad Católica del Perú, Lima, 1984.

——. *Segunda Parte de la crónica del Perú, que trata del señorío de los Incas Yupanqui,* 1554. Reprint: Ed. Manuel González de la Rosa, London, 1873.

——. *Tercera parte, Descubrimiento y Conquista,* ca. 1554. Reprint: Ed. Rafael Loredo, Mercurio Peruano, Books I and II, Lima, 1946.

Cobo, Bernabé. *Historia del Nuevo Mundo,* 1653. Reprint: Editorial Luis A. Pardo, Cuzco, 1956.

Conklin, William J. "Chavin Textiles and the Origins of Peruvian Weaving," *Textile Museum Journal,* Vol. 3, No. 2, Washington, D.C., 1971, pp. 13–19.

——. "An Introduction to South American Archeological Textiles with Emphasis on Materials and Techniques of Peruvian Tapestry," *Irene Emery Roundtable on Museum Textiles, 1974 Proceedings, Archeological Textiles,* Textile Museum, Washington, D.C., 1975, pp. 17–30.

——. "Estructura de los Tejidos Moche," in *Tecnología Andina,* ed. Rogger Ravines, Instituto de Estudios Peruanos, Lima, 1978, pp. 299–333.

——. *Textiles from Ancient Peru: Selections from the Collection of the Peabody Museum, Dumbarton Oaks, Harvard University,* American Federation of the Arts, New York, 1984.

Crawford, M. D. C. "Peruvian Fabrics," *Anthropological Papers of the American Museum of Natural History,* Vol. XII, New York, 1916, pp. 105–91.

——. "Peruvian Textiles," *Anthropological Papers of the American Museum of Natural History,* Vol. XII, New York, 1916, pp. 52–104.

Dawson, Lawrence E. "Painted Cloth Mummy Masks of Ica, Peru," in *Junius B. Bird Pre-Columbian Textile Conference,* Textile Museum, Washington, D.C., 1979, pp. 83–103.

Dockstader, Frederick J. *Indian Art in South America. Pre-Columbian Arts and Crafts,* New York Graphic Society, Greenwich, Conn., 1967.

Dwyer, Jane P. *Iconography and Chronology in Paracas and Nasca Textiles,* University of California, Berkeley, 1971.

Emery, Irene. *The Primary Structures of Fabrics: An Illustrated Classification,* Textile Museum, Washington, D.C., 1966.

Engel, Frédéric. *Paracas: Cién Siglos de Cultura Peruana,* Editorial Juan Mejía Baca, Lima, 1966.

Estete, Miguel de. *The Narrative of the Journey made by Captain Hernando Pizarro, by order of the governor, his brother, from the city of Caxamalca to Parcama and thence to Xauxa,* included in Francisco de Xeres, *Verdadera Relación de la conquista del Perú,* translated and edited by Clements R. Markham, in *Reports on the Discovery of Peru,* Hakluyt Society, London, 1872. Reprint: Plata Publishing Ltd, Chur, Switzerland, n.d., pp. 74–109.

Garcilaso de la Vega, Inca. *Primera Parte de los Comentarios Reales de los Incas,* Lisbon, 1609, and *Segunda Parte de los Comentarios Reales de los Incas: Historia General del Perú,* Córdoba, 1617. Reprint: *Comentarios Reales de los Incas,* 2 vols., Ediciones Peisa, Lima, Peru, 1973. Translated as *The Incas,* ed. Alain Gheerbrant, Avon Library, New York, 1976.

Gayton, Ann. "Significado Cultural de los Tejidos Peruanos: Producción, Función y Belleza," in *Tecnología Andina,* ed. Rogger Ravines, Instituto de Estudios Peruanos, Lima, 1978, pp. 269–99.

Goldwater, Robert. *Primitivism in Modern Art,* 1938. Reprint: Knopf & Random House, New York, 1967.

Harcourt, Raoul d'. *Les Tissus Indiens du Vieux Pérou,* Documents d'Art, Editions Albert Morancé, Paris, 1924.

——. *Les Textiles anciens du Pérou et leurs techniques,* Les Editions d'Art et d'Histoire, Paris, 1934. Translated as *Textiles of Ancient Peru and Their Techniques,* edited by Grace Denny and Carolyn Osborne, University of Washington Press, Seattle, 1962.

Hemming, John. *The Conquest of the Incas,* Harcourt, Brace, Jovanovich, New York, 1970.

Humboldt, Alexander von, and Bonpland, A. *Vues des Cordillères et monuments des peuples indigènes de l'Amérique,* 2 vols., Paris, 1816–24.

Izumi, Seiichi. *Treasures of the Pre-Inca Cultures,* San-Ichi Shobo, Tokyo, 1964.

Kelemen, Pál. *Medieval American Art,* Vol. 2, Dover Publications, Inc., 1969.

King, Mary Elizabeth. *Ancient Peruvian Textiles from the Collection of the Textile Museum, Washington, D.C.,* Museum of Primitive Art, New York, 1965.

——. "A Brief History of the Study of Ancient Peruvian Textiles," *Textile Museum Journal,* III: 1, Washington, D.C., December 1966, pp. 39–44.

Kunisuke, Akashi. *Textiles of Pre-Inca from Burial Grounds in Peru* (the Kanegafuchi collection), 12 vols., published privately by Kanegafuchi, Kyoto, Japan, 1965.

Lapiner, Alan. *Pre-Columbian Art of South America,* Harry N. Abrams Co., New York, 1974.

Lehmann, Walther, and Doering, Heinrich. *Historia del Arte del Antiguo Perú,* Gustavo Gili, Barcelona, 1926.

Lumbreras, Luis Guillermo. *De los Pueblos, las Culturas y las Artes del Antiguo Perú,* Moncloa-Campodónico, Editores Asociados, Lima, 1969.

Marcoy, Paul. *A Journey Across South America,* 4 half-vols., Blackie and Son, London and Glasgow, 1872.

Markham, Clements R. *Reports on the Discovery of Peru* (translation and editing of narratives, accounts and letters of Francisco de Xeres, Miguel de Estete, Hernando Pizarro and Pedro Sancho), Hakluyt Society, London, 1872. Reprint: Plata Publishing Ltd, Chur, Switzerland, n.d.

Mead, Charles W. "Conventionalized Figures in Ancient Peruvian Art," *Anthropological Papers of the American Museum of Natural History*, Vol. XII, New York, 1916, pp. 193–219.

Menzel, Dorothy; Rowe, John H.; and Dawson, Lawrence E. *The Paracas Pottery of Ica: A Study in Style and Time*, University of California Publications in American Archaeology and Ethnology, Vol. 50, Berkeley, 1964.

Middendorf, E. W. *Peru. Beobachtungen und Studien über das Land und seine Bewohner während eines 25jährigen Aufenthalts*, 3 vols., Berlin, 1893–95.

Molina, Cristóbal de (of Cuzco). *Relación de las Fábulas y Ritos de los Incas*, 1573. Trans. C. R. Markham as *The Fables and Rites of the Incas*, Hakluyt Society, No. 48, London, 1873.

Murra, John V. "La Función del Tejido en Varios Contextos Sociales y Políticos," 1958; published in *Formaciones Económicas y Políticas del Mundo Andino*, Instituto de Estudios Peruanos, Lima, pp. 145–70. Translated as "Cloth and Functions in the Inca State," *American Anthropologist*, Vol. 64, No. 4, American Anthropological Association, Menasha, 1962, pp. 71 ff.

Ondegardo, Juan Polo de. *Relación de los Fundamentos acerca del Notable Daño que resulta de no guardar a los indios sus Fueras*, 1571. Reprint: Colección Libros y Documentos, Historia del Perú, Serie 1, Tomo 3, Lima, 1916–17.

O'Neale, Lila M., and Kroeber, A. L. *Textile Periods in Ancient Peru*, University of California Publications in American Archaeology and Ethnology, Vol. 28, No. 2, Berkeley, 1930, pp. 23–56.

O'Neill, John. "Featherwork," in *Costumes and Featherwork of the Lords of Chimor, Textiles from Peru's North Coast*, Textile Museum, Washington, D.C., 1984, pp. 145–94.

Orbigny, Alcide d'. *L'homme Américain de l'Amérique Méridionale, considéré sous ses rapports physiologiques et moraux*, 2 vols., Paris, 1839.

Pineda, Rosa Fung. "Análisis tecnológico de Encajes del antiguo Perú," in *Tecnología Andina*, ed. Rogger Ravines, Instituto de Estudios Peruanos, Lima, 1978, pp. 333–47.

Pizarro, Hernando. *Carta a los magníficos señores, los señores oidores de Audiencia real de S. M. que reside en la ciudad de Santo Domingo*. Translated as *Letter to the Royal Audience of Santo Domingo, 23 November 1533*, by Clements R. Markham, Hakluyt Society, London, 1872. Reprint: Plata Publishing Ltd, Chur, Switzerland, n.d., pp. 113–26.

Pizarro, Pedro. *Relación del Descubrimiento y Conquista de los Reinos del Perú*, 1571, Biblioteca de Autores Españoles (BAE) 168, Editorial M. Menéndez Pelayo, Madrid, 1965, pp. 159 ff.

Poma de Ayala, Felipe Guaman. *El Primer Nueva Corónica y Buen Gobierno*, ca. 1587–1615. Reprint: Siglo Veintiuno Argentina Editores, Buenos Aires, 3 vols., 1980.

Posnansky, Arthur. *Tihuanacu, La Cuña del Hombre Americano* and *Tihuanacu, the Cradle of American Man* (combined English/Spanish edition), Ministry of Education, La Paz, Bolivia, in two tomes (Vols. I/II and III/IV), 1957.

Ravines, Rogger (ed.). *Tecnología Andina*, Instituto de Estudios Peruanos, Lima, 1978.

Reid, James W. *Los Tejidos Pre-Colombinos*, Wildenstein, Buenos Aires, 1974, 1976.

——. *Tejidos Pre-Colombinos Pintados*, Banco de Crédito del Perú, L. L. Editores, Lima, 1979.

——. "Wondrous Cloths," *Art News*, New York, February 1980, pp. 102 ff.

——. "Pre-Columbian Textiles: Woven Treasures from the Andean World, Part I: The Background," *Hali: International Journal of Carpets and Textiles*, Vol. 3, No. 1, London, 1980, pp. 41–44.

——. "Pre-Columbian Textiles: Woven Treasures from the Andean World, Part II: Magic, Mystery and Mythology," *Hali*, Vol. 3, No. 2, London, 1980, pp. 116–21.

——. "Ancient Peruvian Textiles: Raiment for the Gods," *Art and Antiques*, New York, July–August 1981, pp. 66–71.

——. *Chancay: El Tejido Chancay*, Banco de Crédito del Perú, L. L. Editores, Lima, 1982.

——. *Huari: Textiles*, Banco de Crédito del Perú, L. L. Editores, Lima, 1984.

——. "To Splendour . . . Geometry and Abstraction in Ancient Peruvian Textiles," *Hali*, Vol. 7, No. 3, London, 1985, pp. 26–34.

——. "Resplendent Plumage: Feather Textiles of Ancient Peru," *Hali*, Vol. 7, No. 4, London, 1985, pp. 48–56.

——. *The Cosmic and the Divine: Textiles of Ancient Peru* (the Bildner Collection), Israel Museum, Jerusalem, 1985.

——. *La Textilería Nasca*, Banco de Crédito del Perú, L. L. Editores, Lima, 1986.

——. *La Textilería del Reino de Chimor*, Banco de Crédito del Perú, L. L. Editores, Lima, 1987.

Reiss, Wilhelm, and Stübel, Alphons. *Das Totenfeld von Ancon in Peru*, 3 vols., Berlin, 1880–87.

Rostworowski de Diez Canseco, María. *Estructuras Andinas del Poder*, Instituto de Estudios Peruanos, Lima, 1983.

Rowe, Ann P. *A Heritage of Color, Textile Traditions of the South Coast of Peru*, Textile Museum, Washington, D.C., May 22–October 21, 1973.

——. "Interlocking Warp and Weft in the Nasca 2 Style," *Textile Museum Journal*, Vol. 3, No. 3, Washington, D.C., 1973, pp. 67–78.

——. *Peruvian Costume: A Weaver's Art*, Textile Museum, Washington, D.C., April 4–August 31, 1974.

——. *Warp-Patterned Weaves of the Andes*, Textile Museum, Washington, D.C., 1977.

——. "Technical Features of Inca Tapestry Tunics," *Textile Museum Journal*, Vol. 17, Washington, D.C., 1978, pp. 5–28.

——. *Costumes and Featherwork of the Lords of Chimor, Textiles from Peru's North Coast* (with feather identifi-

cation by John P. O'Neill), Textile Museum, Washington, D.C., 1984.

Rowe, John Howland. "Absolute Chronology in the Andean Area," *American Antiquity*, Vol. 10, 1945, pp. 265–84.

——. "Standardization in Inca Tapestry Tunics," in *Junius B. Bird Pre-Columbian Textile Conference*, Textile Museum, Washington, D.C., 1979, pp. 239–65.

Sawyer, Alan R. "Painted Nasca Textiles," in *Essays in Pre-Columbian Art and Archeology*, Harvard University Press, Cambridge, Mass., 1961, pp. 129–51.

——. "Paracas and Nasca Iconography," in *Essays in Pre-Columbian Art and Archeology*, Harvard University Press, Cambridge, Mass., 1961, pp. 269–98.

——. *Tiahuanaco Tapestry Design*, Museum of Primitive Art, New York, 1963.

Squier, Ephraim George. *Peru: Incidents of Travel and Exploration in the Land of the Incas*, Macmillan and Co., London, 1877, and Harper and Brothers, New York, 1877. Translated as *Un Viaje por Tierras Incaicas, Crónica de una expedición arqueológica, 1863–65*, Editorial Los Amigos del Libro, La Paz and Cochabamba, Bolivia, 1974.

Strand, Mark. *18 Poems from the Quechua*, Halty Ferguson, Cambridge, Mass., 1971.

Strong, William D. *Paracas, Nasca, and Tiahuanacoid Cultural Relationships in South Coastal Peru*, Memoirs of the Society for American Archeology, No. 13, Salt Lake City, Utah, 1957.

Taullard, Alfredo. *Tejidos y Ponchos Indígenas de Sudamérica*, Editorial Guillermo Kraft, Buenos Aires, 1949.

Tello, Julio C. *Wiracocha*, Inca Revista de Estudios Antropológicos, Universidad Nacional Mayor de San Marcos, Vol. II, Primera Parte, Lima, 1923.

——. *Los Descubrimientos del Museo de Arqueología Peruana en la Península de Paracas*, XXII Congreso Internacional de Americanistas, Primera Parte, Rome, 1928.

——. *Origen y Desarrollo de las Civilizaciones Pre-Hispánicas Andinas*, Lima, 1942.

——. *Paracas, Primera Parte*, Universidad Nacional Mayor de San Marcos and the Museo Nacional de Antropología y Arqueología, Lima, 1959.

Uhle, Max. *Los Orígenes de los Incas*, Proceedings, 17th International Congress of Americanists, I, Buenos Aires, 1910, pp. 230–53.

——. *Die alten Kulturen Perus im Hinblick auf die Archaeologie und Geschichte des amerikanischen Kontinents*, Berlin, 1935.

——. *Los Geroglifos de la Portada de Tiahuanacu*, XXV Congreso Internacional de Americanistas.

Valcarcel, Luis E. "La Religión Incaica," in *Historia del Perú, Tomo III: Perú Antiguo*, Editorial Juan Mejía Baca, Lima, 1980 (reprint, 1981), pp. 75–202.

Van Stan, Ina. *The Fabrics of Peru*, F. Lewis, Leigh-on-Sea (England), 1966.

Versteylen, Eduardo C. *Técnicas Textiles del Valle de Chancay*, Universidad Nacional Mayor de San Marcos, Lima, 1971.

Von Hagen, Victor. *The Desert Kingdoms of Peru*, Weidenfeld and Nicholson, London, 1965.

Wallace, Dwight T. "The Process of Weaving Development on the Peruvian Coast," in *Junius B. Bird Pre-Columbian Textile Conference*, Textile Museum, Washington, D.C., 1979, pp. 27–51.

Wiener, Charles. *Pérou et Bolivie: Récit de Voyage*, Librairie Hachette, Paris, 1880.

Xeres, Francisco de. *Verdadera Relación de la Conquista del Perú y Provincia del Cuzco, llamada la Nueva Castilla*, Seville, 1534; second edition, Salamanca, 1547. Translated and edited as *A True Account of the Province of Cuzco called New Castille*, in *Reports on the Discovery of Peru* by Clements R. Markham, Hakluyt Society, London, 1872. Reprint: Plata Publishing Ltd, Chur, Switzerland, n.d., pp. 1–71.

Yacovleff, Eugenio, and Herrera, Fortunato L. "El Mundo Vegetal de los Antiguos Peruanos," *Revista del Museo Nacional de Lima*, III, 1934, pp. 241–322; IV, No. 1, 1935, pp. 29–102.

Zarate, Agustín de. *Historia del Descubrimiento y Conquista del Peru*, Antwerp, 1555; reprint, Seville, 1577. Translated by T. Nicholas, London, 1581, and as *History of the Discovery and Conquest of Peru* by J. M. Cohen, Harmondsworth (England), 1968.

FIGURATIVE MOTIFS

1. Paracas, South Coast, Ocucaje region, ca. 300–100 B.C. Mummy bundle of plain weave, undyed natural cotton painted with the symmetrical frontal design of a deity flanked by upright serpentiform zigzag motifs. 13 × 15 inches. (In all dimensions, height precedes width.)

Plate 1

2

Plate 2

2. Paracas Necropolis, South Coast, ca. 700–100 B.C. Embroidered mantle, consisting of a central blue area, on which appear 37 figures, and a red border, on which are depicted additional figures. The main motifs are probably shamans eulogizing or invoking the gods. Some are winged, and all appear to have their faces painted or to wear fantastic masks. They carry either trophy heads, weapons or what may be the branch of a plant or tree. 58 × 114 inches.

Plate 3

3. Paracas Necropolis, South Coast, ca. 700–100 B.C. Embroidered wool mantle depicting figures that appear to be either falling or flying, with hair trailing behind them, *tumi*-type knives in their hands and a bewhiskered feline visage surmounting their forehead. Complete mantle: 52 × 101 inches.

Plate 4

4

4. Paracas Necropolis, South Coast, ca. 600–100 B.C. *Esclavina* (small mantle) of cotton, embroidered in wool with alternating upright and inverted condors carrying a miniature whale in their claws. 24 × 34 inches. **5.** Paracas Necropolis, South Coast, ca. 600–100 B.C. Mantle with wool ground of deep blue embroidered with alternating images of upright and inverted condors. Similar smaller figures appear on the red border. 40 × 82 inches.

5

Plate 5

6

6. Paracas Necropolis, South Coast, ca. 600–100 B.C. Wool mantle embroidered with mystical anthropomorphic figures carrying trophy heads and fruits and forming a checkerboard pattern. 45 × 91 inches. **7.** Paracas Necropolis, South Coast, ca. 600–100 B.C. Detail of an embroidered wool mantle of characteristic checkerboard design. The embroidered squares and border area contain one of the most extraordinary mythological composite beings in the Paracas lexicon of fantastic creatures. Serpents, condors and supernatural fanged images of Chavinoid aspect constitute the main appendages; they emanate from the head as whiskers or claws, and create a mood of untrammeled fantasy which can only seem surrealist to the twentieth-century mind. Complete mantle: 45 × 96 inches. **8.** Paracas Necropolis, South Coast, ca. 600–100 B.C. Detail of a cotton mantle with woolen border. The main field area of the mantle contains broad bands of red, yellow and blue-green. The detail depicts one of the border figures. He carries a trophy head, his body contains miniature trophy heads, his legs convert into trophy heads and he is flanked laterally by larger trophy heads. Complete mantle: 58 × 120 inches. **9.** Paracas Necropolis, South Coast, ca. 600–100 B.C. Detail of a wool mantle with areas of plain old-gold yellow alternating with embroidered images in a checkerboard configuration. The figures are human, but with claw-like feet and tongues that become serpents. The headdress is an elaborate conical diadem with an extension that appears to be a centipede terminating in a trophy head. Complete mantle: 52 × 102 inches.

Plate 6

7

8

9

Plate 7

The concept of dualism was an omnipresent one in much of the practical, philosophical and iconographic life of ancient Peru. The Incas used dualism extensively in their administration: cities had upper and lower areas, units had two commanders and gods possessed dark and light sides to their personalities. The philosophic facet of dualism was best reflected in two Quechua words, *yanantin* and *yanapaque*, which referred generally to mirror imagery and bodily symmetry, and to the idea of the shadow, or helper, of a specific person.

In textile iconography, dualism is manifested through bicephalic figures (bodies with heads at both extremities) and dual renditions of the same motif. The latter characteristic is illustrated in the two examples on this page. In both cases, motifs of similar shape and size, but with different colors, are shown in opposite configurations as examples of what the Israeli sociologist Dr. Trion Avital has termed "transformation conversion."

10

11

10. Nasca, South Coast, ca. 200 B.C.–800 A.D. Interlocking warp and weft tapestry *cushma* (sleeveless shirt) depicting two large anthropomorphic figures with frog-like attributes. 60 × 30 inches.   **11.** Nasca, South Coast, ca. 200 B.C.–800 A.D. Interlocking warp and weft tapestry *cushma* depicting two large figures resembling bats. 70 × 39 inches.

Plate 8

12

12. Nasca, South Coast, ca. 200 B.C.–300 A.D. Detail of a *llautu* or *turbante* (headband) depicting a spider with extended legs. Complete *llautu:* 13 × 46 inches.   **13.** Nasca, South Coast, ca. 200 B.C.–400 A.D. *Cushma* (sleeveless shirt) with each side containing four winged dragons rendered in a stylized geometric manner. 30 × 30 inches.

13

Plate 9

14

14. Nasca–Huari, South Coast, ca. 700–1100 A.D. Tabard of natural cotton with appliqué small red, blue and yellow feathers of the guacamayo macaw, and larger salmon-colored feathers of the flamingo. The dramatic visual appeal of the piece is due to the unusual combination of a *tumi*-type knife, two bicephalic dragons and radiant suns whose facial expressions suggest twentieth-century Expressionist overtones. The sun motif is characteristic of Nasca–Huari feather textiles and is generally depicted with eight rays, less commonly with six. 58 × 38 inches.

16. Nasca, South Coast, ca. 300–700 A.D. Cotton panel, embellished with feathers, depicting a starfish. 24 × 29 inches.

16

Plate 10

Themes related to the sky, the sea and the earth are omnipresent reminders of the synergistic ties that kept the ancient Peruvian in contact with the world around him and with its deities. His world was a pantheistic one of immanent divine presences: the sun, supreme celestial deity, and the two-headed dragon, symbol of rain and tempests. The starfish, only one of the numerous manifestations of marine life, imposes itself across the whole surface texture with rhythmic power. From the earth, from the tropical lowlands to the east of the Andes, the monkey appears, as though in a macabre dance. Surging out of a fiery background of smouldering vermilion, the looming figure epitomizes the primeval incarnation of an atavistic past and a catalytic, dynamic life-force.

15

15. Detail of Illus. 14.

17. Nasca, South Coast, ca. 100–800 A.D. Cotton panel with applied feathers portraying the frontal image of a monkey in motion. 22 × 29 inches.

17

Plate 11

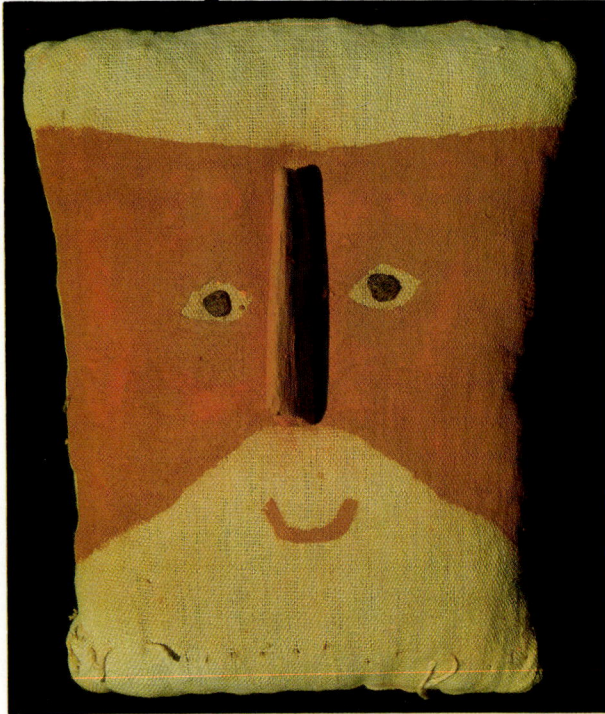

18

Facial effigies, as masks or pillows, are omnipresent in ancient Peruvian textile art. Such masks as those in Illus. 19 and 20 generally covered either the head of the person buried in the funeral bundle or the trophy head of a vanquished enemy.

20

19

18. Chancay, Central Coast, ca. 1000–1460 A.D. Pillow of totora reeds enclosed in cotton, with a painted face in frontal view. 14 inches high.   19. Nasca–Huari, South Coast, ca. 700–1000 A.D. Tears—a Huari convention whose origin may be traced to the weeping central figure on the Tiahuanaco stone frieze denominated the Gateway of the Sun—are represented by vertical lines of yellow feathers. The cloth was used to tie up a trophy head. 10 inches high.   20. Nasca–Huari, South Coast, ca. 700–1000 A.D. Mask of natural cotton to which feathers were applied with a paste made from maize. It was placed over a trophy head. The eyes, delineated with a black line and with a vertical as the pupil, are characteristic of Nasca; the grid-like mouth is another Huari convention. 10 inches high.

Plate 12

21

Elaborate vestments and accessories, in both the figurative and nonfigurative genres, created spectacular panoplies of brilliant color and coruscating surfaces, as shown by these three illustrations.

22

23

21. Chimu, North Coast, ca. 1000–1460 A.D. Ceremonial crown of leather adorned with feathers. The hands, which hold what appear to be cotton bolls, have converted into zoomorphic heads. 4 × 14 inches.   **22.** Nasca, South Coast, ca. 100–800 A.D. Cotton tabard with applied feathers representing 16 birds repeated in a serial-imagery pattern. 56 × 38 inches.   **23.** Chimu, North Coast, ca. 1000–1460 A.D. Ceremonial shoulder vestment of natural cotton embellished with feathers and made to be tied loosely around the neck so that the piece covers the back down to the waist. The "barry" design consists of horizontal bands of white, orange and cerulean blue guaca-mayo macaw feathers, with longer umber-colored condor feathers superimposed upon the top band. 30 × 20 inches.

Plate 13

24. Nasca, South Coast, ca. 100–800
A.D. Cotton tabard with applied
feathers. This textile is unusual for
the inclusion of tarantulas, a rare
theme in textile imagery. 74 × 37
inches. **25.** Nasca–Huari, South
Coast, ca. 700–1000 A.D. Cotton
tabard with applied feathers. The
central segment, which would fall
over the shoulders when worn, is
left plain. One half of the tabard
contains three imposing deity figures with unusually dramatic facial
expressions; the other half contains
geometric motifs. 60 × 32 inches.

Plate 14

25

Plate 15

26. Chimu, North Coast, ca. 1000–1460 A.D. Tapestry panel depicting the moon dragon as a focal central image, with stylized caymans above and below. In ancient Peruvian textiles, the moon goddess Si is also found represented in ornithomorphic form. 24 × 29 inches.

Plate 16

27. Nasca, South Coast, ca. 200 B.C.–300 A.D. Front half of a closely woven *cushma* (sleeveless shirt) of wool looping, showing a monumental kneeling monkey with body in profile and face in frontal view. Monkeys are associated with the Amazonian tropical lowlands and, like such animals as the cayman, evidently became well known to the coastal peoples, who incorporated these jungle denizens into their iconography. 27 × 38 inches. **28.** Late Huari–Early Chimu, North Coast, ca. 800–1100 A.D. Natural dark brown cotton panel painted with a large spotted feline with oversize whiskers and curvilinear tail. 36 × 42 inches.

27

28

Plate 17

29. Paracas, South Coast, ca. 500–200 B.C. Segment of a mantle of cream-colored natural cotton painted with recurring images of a type of jellyfish (*pota* or *malagua*) with downward-extending tentacles. The motif is similar to the hand theme often used in ancient Peruvian textiles. The dots may signify grains of sand, with the composition possibly representing a graphic depiction of homage to the sea. 40 × 42 inches.

30

30. Chancay, Central Coast, ca. 1000–1460 A.D. Mantle of natural brown cotton embroidered with a symmetrical repeat pattern of large coiled two-headed snakes. 60 × 40 inches.

"They worshipped . . . large snakes for their ferocity and monstrous size . . . of up to 25 or 30 feet" (Inca Garcilaso de la Vega, *Comentarios Reales de los Incas*, Tome I, Book 1, p. 36).

"Then he [Huallallo] created an immense two-headed serpent called Amaru. . . . 'That ought to terrify the god Pariacaca,' said Huallallo" (anonymous author, late sixteenth century, *Dioses y Hombres de Huarochiri*, Siglo XXI Editores, Mexico City, 1975, p. 80).

"The two-headed snake is associated with rain, fertility and agricultural growth. Lightning is incarnated in the serpent, which symbolizes rain and fertility of the earth. The serpent is the rainbow, as well as being a *waraka* (whip-like sling) which the gods wield to create rain. . . . It also appears periodically . . . as the Pleiades" (Rebeca Carrión Cachot de Girard, *La Religión en el Antiguo Perú*, Lima, 1959, pp. 14, 29).

Plate 18

31. Ychma–Pachacamac, Central Coast, Lurín valley area, ca. 1000–1532 A.D. *Cushma* (sleeveless shirt), cotton and wool, depicting fish which appear to be plaice, flounder or sole. 45 × 52 inches.

"In different provinces and regions, they worshipped the fish of which they caught the greatest quantities . . . because they said that the first fish to exist . . ., which was the progenitor of subsequent species, took care to send them abundant numbers of his sons for their alimentary needs; and so in some provinces they worshipped the sardine, in others the skate and the spotted dogfish" (Inca Garcilaso de la Vega, *Comentarios Reales de los Incas*, Tome I, Book 1, Chap. X, p. 37).

Garcilaso also recounts that, prior to the Inca conquest of the coast in the mid-fifteenth century, the ruler of six central coast river valleys, including Pachacamac and Chancay, was Cuismancu; and that Cuismancu's ancestors built the temple of Ychma (later called Pachacamac by the Incas) and placed in it "their idols, which were images of fishes, and also of foxes" (Tome II, Book 6, Chap. XXX, p. 179).

Plate 19

32

33

32. Chimu, North Coast, ca. 1000–1460 A.D. Wool and cotton panel depicting six frontal deities truncated at the waist. Their arms seem to end in bat claws. The deities appear above fishing boats known as *caballitos*. Still used today in such fishing ports as Huanchaco, near Trujillo, they are constructed of totora reeds and weigh approximately 300 pounds. 30 × 60 inches.   **33.** Chimu, Central Coast, ca. 1000–1460 A.D. Ceremonial pillow of cotton and wool originally padded with a thin layer of cotton and backed by a light gauze. Each of the 15 frontal deity figures—which may represent Con, Naylamp or Cuismancu—is surrounded by four guardian monkeys in a squatting posture. 23 × 31 inches.

Plate 20

The processes of what Robert Goldwater has called "intellectual realism" (the deliberate exaggeration of the size of certain parts of the body), of fragmentation (the breaking up or truncating of corporeal elements) and of dislocation (the arbitrary placing of segments of the body in the design so as to conform with compositional dictates rather than with anatomical realism) are omnipresent characteristics of ancient Peruvian iconography. The simplest form of fragmentation is illustrated by the truncated figures shown in Illus. 32; abbreviated at the waist, they contrast notably with the more conventional deity figures shown in Illus. 33 and 34. More complex and elaborate fragmentation and dislocation can be found in Tiahuanaco and Huari textiles.

34. Chimu, North Coast, ca. 1000–1460 A.D. Cotton and wool shirt portraying deity figures—possibly Con, Naylamp or Cuismancu—surrounded by deer. Deer are rarely portrayed in textiles. In this textile two separate panels, with similar iconographic motifs but with slight differences in warp and weft structure, were joined together to form a shirt. Such panels, although destined for the same vestment, were probably made by different weavers working in the same area. 38 × 40 inches.

Plate 21

Plate 22

35. Chancay, Central Coast, ca. 1000–1460 A.D.
Mantle consisting of 24 panels of varying
shades of natural cotton on 12 of which are
embroidered symmetrical frontal deity figures wearing characteristic crescent headdress and earplugs and a vestment containing
horizontal scroll motifs. 81 × 91 inches.

Plate 23

36

36. Paracas–Proto-Nasca, South Coast, ca. 200 B.C.–100 A.D. Embroidered wool mantle consisting of a main gray field on which are embroidered flowers. The red border contains fantastic figures with elaborate headdresses. 44 × 109 inches.   **37.** Chancay, Central Coast, ca. 1000–1460 A.D. Cotton mantle embroidered with wool motifs of a cormorant presented in a serial-imagery pattern. 56 × 98 inches.

37

Plate 24

Serial imagery, the repeated rendition of one motif of uniform size, and of either identical or varying colors, is an artistic convention constantly employed by ancient Peruvian textile artists. The themes portrayed were invariably subjects of awe and veneration, so that their repetition represented both homage to the gods and wonders of nature and a visual reminder of the significance of such motifs in daily life. Illus. 32–35 depict anthropomorphic figures, deities or god impersonators. The themes illustrated here—flowers, feather plumes and the guanay cormorant (source of the indispensable guano)—focus on the world of flora and fauna.

38

38. Chimu, North Coast, ca. 1000–1450 A.D. Detail, 30 × 36 inches, of a mantle consisting of four tapestry panels of cotton warp and wool weft. The design is of characteristic yellow plumes on a muted geranium-lake background, with upper and lower selvedges containing a continuous register of scroll (wave) symbols, and with lateral selvedges of woven deity figures surmounted with crescent-type headdress. Complete mantle 72 × 112 inches.

Plate 25

39

39. Huari, South Highland, ca. 300–800 A.D. Painted design on cotton of a central frontal deity flanked by profile figures. 26 × 60 inches.   **40.** Chancay, Central Coast, ca. 1000–1460 A.D. Detail of a cotton mantle painted with approximately 900 deity figures accompanied by ornate discs that appear to be shields. The piece reportedly enveloped a female dignitary of high rank. 54 × 252 inches.

40

Plate 26

Ancient Peruvian artists painted directly onto unprimed cotton. Their themes included monumental motifs, of the types shown in Illus. 39 and 41; huge compositions of identical figures, like the warrior deities with shields represented more than 900 times in the colossal mantle shown in Illus. 40; and complex rhythmic patterns formed of strange creatures of the type shown in Illus. 42.

41. Tiahuanaco, South Altiplano, ca. 300–800 A.D. Cotton panel painted with the image of a large running *chasqui* messenger figure, with appendages that end in serpent or llama heads. The main figure is flanked by stylized trophy heads. 38 × 42 inches.   42. Paracas, South Coast, ca. 800–500 B.C. Detail of a large mantle painted in umber browns on a cream background and depicting creatures with centipede/serpent attributes and with faces having dramatically rounded large eyes associated with the "Oculate Being," a figure that permeates much of Paracas and Nasca imagery. Complete mantle: 75 × 120 inches.

Plate 27

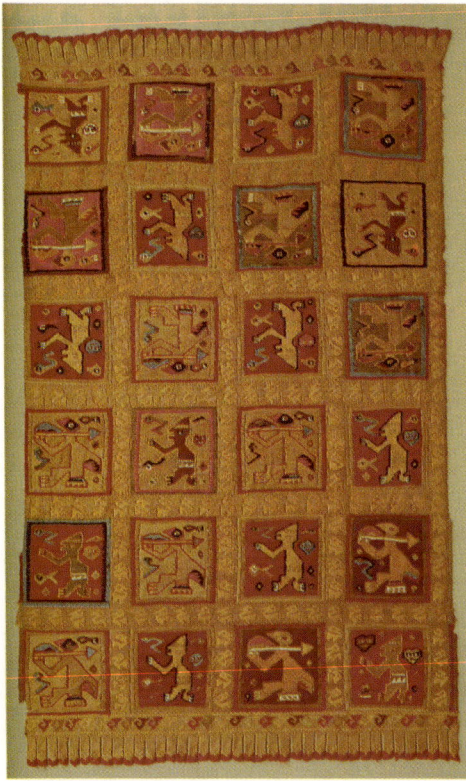

43

43. Late Huari–Early Chancay, Central Coast, ca. 800–1100 A.D. Wool panel depicting unusually conceived figures. 27 × 18 inches. **44.** Chancay, Central Coast, ca. 1000–1460 A.D. Cotton and wool mantle composed of an allover surface design in which felines are the predominant motif. 70 × 62½ inches.

44

Plate 28

45

45. Pachacamac, Central Coast, ca. 1000–1530 A.D. Shirt (opened up) depicting two-headed figures, with borders of stylized birds. 30 × 34 inches. **46.** Chancay, Central Coast near Paramonga, ca. 1000–1460 A.D. Mantle consisting of three natural brown cotton panels embroidered with undulating zigzag lines of upright and inverted stylized heads and arms. The combination of red, rose, violet and yellow is unusual in central coast textiles. 48 × 64 inches.

46

Plate 29

Ancient Peruvian weavers exploited endlessly the infinite graphic possibilities of an extremely limited repertory of motifs, as shown in the two Huari textiles in Illus. 47 and 48. In the *unku*, the silhouette-like form of the profiled winged *chasqui* messenger figure offers opportunities for lyrical experiments in graphic design. The eye, for example, appears frequently as the head of a surrealistic figure combining the attributes of an amoebic, tadpole-like creature and a wraithlike phantom. In the *cushma*, the profiled figures are more traditional. The eye is a bisected disc, the mouth a rectangle whose N design may symbolize the fangs of a feline, and the hands and feet are delineated in stark, dark lines that presage the Huari stylized grid symbol. The overall design is structured by vertical columns of chevrons, a favorite Huari motif. Such textiles probably reached the coast through trade or religious contacts.

47

47. Huari, North Coast, ca. 300–800 A.D. *Unku* (tunic with sleeves), wool and cotton. 37 × 58 inches.

Plate 30

48. Huari, South Coast, ca. 300–800 A.D. *Cushma* (sleeveless shirt), wool and cotton. 41 × 46 inches.

Plate 31

49

49. Huari, North Coast, Huarmey area, ca. 600–1000 A.D. *Cushma,* wool and cotton. 36 × 40 inches.

Plate 32

Stylization, both simple and complex, is a marked characteristic of figurative themes in Tiahuanaco and Huari textile iconography. In Illus. 50, the trophy heads and butterflies—the latter being a singularly rare topic in Peruvian weaving—are reduced to simplified formats that are immediately recognizable. In the case of Illus. 49, however, the highly complex profile figures are so intricately integrated into the surrounding area that they become totally assimilated into the allover two-dimensional surface design. Such iconography is only a step away from the passage into nonfigurative compositions.

50

50. Huari, South Highland, ca. 300–800 A.D. *Cushma,* wool and cotton. 41 × 42 inches.

Plate 33

SYMBOLISM: PICTOGRAPHS AND IDEOGRAMS

51. Huarmey (Huari influence), North Coast, ca. 800–1200 A.D. Sleeveless shirt of wool, tapestry technique. The vertical bands of pure color and of stylized symbols are separate entities and are sewn together to form a composite piece. The border contains 22 warrior deities on each side, richly attired with elaborate headdresses and carrying trophy heads. The brilliant geranium-lake red is of an unusual intensity. 30 × 61 inches.

Plate 34

51

Plate 35

52

52. Huari, North Coast, ca. 300–800 A.D. Detail of a wool and cotton shirt with repeated renditions of a truncated profile figure consisting of a head and outstretched arm with three fingers. Detail: 8 × 8 inches. Complete shirt: 42 × 46 inches. **53.** Huari, North Coast, ca. 300–1000 A.D. *Cushma* (sleeveless shirt) of cotton and wool. Of special interest in this tunic is the *trompe-l'œil* effect of the monkey-deity faces, whose dual frontal and profile posture suggests an affinity with the works of such twentieth-century Cubist painters as Juan Gris. 38 × 40 inches.

53

Plate 36

The transition from highly stylized figurative motifs to more abstract nonfigurative symbols can be clearly traced stylistically, especially in tapestry textiles. For example, the grid motif that appears in Illus. 54 is a simplification of what were once realistic elements—hands, fingers, feet, wings, etc.—outlined in stark dark tones and originally constituting integral elements of complete figure representations. This use of nonfigurative imagery as a graphic symbol—as opposed to the decorative allover surfaces characteristic of Nasca south coast textiles—achieves its apotheosis in Inca tapestry weaving.

54

54. Huari, South Coast, ca 600–1000 A.D. *Cushma*. Interlocked tapestry, cotton warp and alpaca weft. 42 × 40 inches.

Plate 37

55

55. Huari, South Coast, ca. 700–1000 A.D. Shirt, interlocked tapestry with cotton warps and alpaca wefts, consisting of vertical bands of plain yellow ocher color that alternate with bands containing characteristic Huari symbols: bisected-disc eyes with tear pendant, rectangles with interlocking V designs which may symbolize feline fangs, and a paired step-volute motif. As with virtually all Huari shirts of this type, designs are identical on both front and back of the shirt; the piece was made by joining together two panels the length of which was approximately four times the width, an area in the center being left open to accommodate the head. 40 × 39 inches. **56.** Inca, South Coast, ca. 1400–1532 A.D. Tunic in cotton and wool. The *tocapu* square designs contain the symbol for the Quechua word *kapak*, which means noble, lord or august sovereign. In such Inca tunics, the lower segment is characteristically composed of broad horizontal bands of alternating colors. 38 × 32 inches.

56

Of all the ancient Peruvian cultures, the Incas least used realistic and figurative motifs in their textile iconography. There are exceptions: depictions of felines, human/deity figures, groups of interlocking avian designs contained within small rectangles, etc. However, the Incas generally favored, in their characteristic tapestry weaves, pictograms and symbols, or such geometric shapes as the square and the diamond.

Plate 38

57. Inca, Southern Highlands, ca 1400–1532 A.D. Wool shirt depicting a V-neck design with *tocapu* ideograms, ten trophy heads in the upper half of the piece and 12 adornments in the lower area. This textile, found some 30 miles from Cuzco, is one of the few known major textiles to be found in a mountain cave. "With regard to those in the highlands . . . they worship the jaguar (*otorongo*), which they call *otorongo achachi yaya* (grandfather, ancestor) . . . and for this reason the Inca ruler wished to be known as *Otorongo Achachi Ynga*, the Inca Jaguar" (Felipe Guaman Poma de Ayala, *Nueva Crónica*, Tome I, p. 243). 28 × 36 inches.

Plate 39

NONFIGURATIVE AND ABSTRACT COMPOSITIONS

58

58. Nasca–Huari, South Coast, ca. 700–1000 A.D. Mantle. Such tie-dyed textiles, which tend to combine Huari highland techniques with Nasca coastal colors, are the most dramatic example of "abstract art in motion" in all of ancient Peru. 124 × 76 inches.

Plate 40

59. Nasca, South Coast, ca. 200 B.C.–800 A.D. Detail of a *cushma* (sleeveless shirt) in which richly embroidered circles in shades of green, yellow and blue contrast lyrically with an opulent carmine background. The textured, three-dimensional effects of the circles suggests an artistic mood evocative of dots in a Van Gogh landscape. Complete *cushma*: 15 × 29 inches. **60.** Nasca, South Coast, ca. 100–800 A.D. Wool mantle with multicolored rectangles in a variation of the conventional checkerboard composition. 71 × 75 inches.

Plate 41

The multiple possibilities of the square and the rectangle as decorative devices were exploited endlessly by ancient Peruvian artists. One such example was the twin-rectangle banner motif, so called because in its basic, most simplified format two color fields are juxtaposed to form a sleeveless shirt that looks like a flag or banner. Design variations occur according to the different peripheral formats employed. In Illus. 62 and 63, the checkerboard and the extended-step motif surround the nuclear design, whereas in Illus. 64, the artist rearranges the compositional elements in a more complex variation.

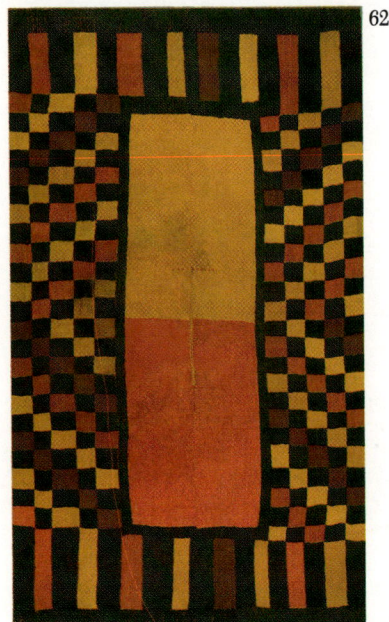

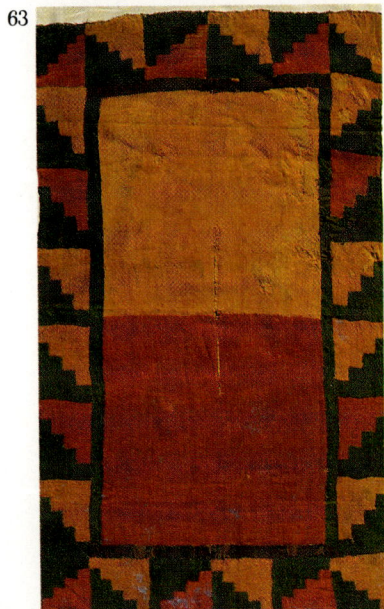

61. Nasca, South Coast, ca. 200 B.C.–800 A.D. *Cushma* (sleeveless shirt), wool and cotton, interlocking warp and weft, basic twin-rectangle design. 78 × 34 inches. **62.** Nasca, South Coast, ca. 200 B.C.–800 A.D. *Cushma*, wool and cotton, interlocking warp and weft. This unusual variation of the twin-rectangle design is notable for the bold vertical colored rectangular bars bordering the more conventional checkerboard motifs. 68 × 40 inches. **63.** Nasca, South Coast, ca. 200 B.C.–800 A.D. *Cushma*, wool and cotton, interlocking warp and weft, basic twin-rectangle design with extended-step periphery. 60 × 40 inches. **64.** Nasca, South Coast, ca. 200 B.C.–800 A.D. *Cushma*, wool and cotton, interlocking warp and weft. The basic twin-rectangle design has undergone considerable modifications, with the artist using a leitmotiv of an X-shaped checkerboard against a background in which the conventional shapes have been rearranged and dispersed. 64 × 33 inches.

Plate 42

65

The evolution of the stripe from an elongated rectangular shape into an elegant formal motif is clearly shown in Illus. 65 and 66. Although the stripe here appears as an integral element of a uniform allover composition, ancient Peruvian artists used it in multiple ways. One of the most dramatic patterns was as a single line bisecting a monochrome color field, or as groups of lines placed on each side of a large mantle of a single color.

66

65. Nasca, South Coast, ca. 200 B.C.–800 A.D. *Awayo* or *llikla* (shawl), wool and cotton, interlocking warp and weft. 30 × 70 inches.   66. Nasca, South Coast, ca. 200 B.C.–800 A.D. *Cushma*, wool. 34 × 38 inches.

Plate 43

67.

68.

67. Nasca, South Coast, ca. 600–800 A.D. Sleeveless shirt consisting of two panels sewn together, with a narrow slit left open in the center to accommodate the head of the wearer. The allover step design used in a zigzag pattern is uncannily modern. The feeling is of rows of skyscrapers thrusting impatiently upward in a landscape mosaic of coruscating blues, geranium lakes and regal golds. 80 × 50 inches. **68.** Nasca, South Coast, ca. 100–800 A.D. Mantle woven of wool and consisting of interlocking step designs forming diagonal patterns within an allover composition. The turquoise-green tonality, chromatically juxtaposed with the geranium red, creates a kaleidoscopic rhythm of color and is a characteristic example of the way in which ancient Peruvian weavers understood the harmony of complementary colors. 60 × 51 inches. **69.** Nasca–Huari, South Coast (Ica Valley), ca. 700–1100 A.D. *Llikla* or *awayo* of wool, with step patterns arranged in a rhythmic harmony of the umbers, madder reds and chrome yellows characteristic of these south coast shawls. 26 × 86 inches. **70.** Nasca–Huari, South Coast, ca. 700–1100 A.D. *Llikla* or *awayo* of wool and cotton, dominated by a massive stepped form that resembles a temple or pyramid, or the dais on which the central deity stands in the Gateway of the Sun frieze at Tiahuanaco. The austere umber shape silhouetted against the off-white ground, which is complemented by white fringes, creates a mood of monumental simplicity akin to that present in certain examples of Minimal Art. 25 × 76 inches. **71.** Proto-Nasca, South Coast, ca. 100 B.C.–100 A.D. Wool mantle. 26 × 47 inches.

Plate 44

69

70

71

Plate 45

Feather textiles, especially those of the south coast, explode with bursts of sumptuous color, evoking the opulent splendor of medieval European heraldry. But no Crusader's richly emblazoned pennant could ever match the spectacular bravura of these visual tours de force from the south coast of ancient Peru. Drenched in nacreous sunlight, their surfaces vary from tactile textures to the delicate, velvet-like sheen of the white ground of the front half of the tabard in Illus. 75.

73

72

72. Huari, South Coast, ca. 700–1000 A.D. Tabard of natural cotton, embellished with blue, yellow and red-orange macaw feathers, depicting on one side what appears to be a gateway motif. 57 × 30 inches. **73.** Nasca, South Coast, ca. 200 B.C.–800 A.D. Tabard of natural tan-colored cotton enriched with yellow, green and red feathers of the macaw and with whitish-pink feathers of the flamingo. 26 × 84 inches.

Plate 46

74

74. Nasca, with Huari influence, South Coast, ca. 700–1000 A.D. Tabard of natural cotton with appliquéd macaw feathers forming a cross-like insignia design. 63 × 26 inches. **75.** Nasca, South Coast, ca. 200 B.C.–800 A.D. Front side of a tabard of natural cotton adorned with feathers. Abstract designs are composed against a white ground. 28 × 26 inches.

75

Plate 47

Textiles of this type were used for objects that were particularly prized by the elite theocratic and secular authorities. They often had unusual significance linked to a specific event. The infant shirt in Illus. 76 is an example of such a cult object; it was reportedly used in the *capocha,* a ceremony initiated by the ninth supreme Inca Pachacuti, who ruled from approximately 1438 to 1463. The Spanish chronicler Cristóbal de Molino of Cuzco recounts that children of between two and twelve years of age were selected for this ritual sacrifice, which appears to have generally occurred at the beginning of the reign of each Inca. The children were amply fed and then given large amounts of coca leaves which, stuffed into their mouths, caused suffocation. The *ataderos* in Illus. 77 are especially rare, the only other comparable piece being in the Rockefeller wing of the Metropolitan Museum of Art in New York.

76

76. Chimu, North Coast, ca. 1000–1460 A.D. Child's *unku* (shirt with sleeves) of natural cream-colored cotton embellished with appliquéd rectangular silver medallions having designs embossed in the repoussé technique, with macaw feathers and with silver pendants along the lower border. 14 × 12 inches. **77.** Chimu, North Coast, ca. 1000–1460 A.D. A pair of ceremonial *ataderos* (anklets/shoes) of natural cream-colored cotton, each one decorated with 72 rectangular appliquéd silver medallions having designs embossed in the repoussé technique. The sole of each shoe is of the same silver. Height of each shoe: 9 inches.

77

Plate 48